The Widow's Mite: A Love Story

The Widow's Mite: A Love Story

(Losing A Love, Finding Another)

Dr. Herldleen Russell

XULON PRESS

Xulon Press
555 Winderley Pl, Suite 225
Maitland, FL 32751
407.339.4217
www.xulonpress.com

Paperback ISBN-13: 978-1-66288-422-1
Ebook ISBN-13: 978-1-66288-423-8

Dedication

A Book is never written by one person, there are so many contributors to it, either in life experiences, teachers/mentors and examples, both good and bad I dedicate this took to each person that has been a part of my life that help write this book.

Glenda Love High my friend of over 60 years…the energizer bunny and my editor. Tawanda Davis, the fire beneath my writing that keeps me on schedule and takes my books to the finish.

<u>The Awesome writers that contributed from their heart in this book</u>

Bishop Carl A. Pierce, Sr.
Pastor Patrick L. Russell
Evangelist Euland R Parker
Evangelist Tekesha Russell
Evangelist Alvera Lewis
Minister Larry Bronson
Mother Dorothy Dyette
Minister Glenda Love High

And He sat down opposite the temple treasure and begun watching how the people were putting money into the treasury. And many rich people were putting in large sums. A poor widow came and put in two small copper coins which amount to a mite. Call His disciples to Him, He said to them, I assure you and most solemnly say to you, this poor widow put in proportionally more than all the contributors to the treasury. For they all contributed from their surplus, but she from her poverty, put in all she had, all she had to live on?

Mark 12: 41-44

Foreword

_____ᏸᏸ _____

We all experience lost in our lives, it's a part of life. What do you do when you lose someone? It can make the difference in the rest of your life.

God has purpose for everything in your life. Could that lost be a part of His purpose...but why does it hurt so bad...when He promises *that everything will work together for their good.*

Come on a journey with me and see some who has lost, but not only did it *work together for their good,* but He did "exceedingly abundantly above all that they could ask or think...."

In the marketplace on the way to the temple, there is a crowd, filing into the temple. Traditionally there is a box placed in front of the entrance for offerings—money to support all of the temple's efforts. Those that have large quantities of money and are clothed in their finery have picked their offerings carefully for maximum melody as it falls into the offering box with loud clinks of sounding brass and tinkling silver.

A widow passes by the box, stoops and places her very small offering in the container. But it was recognized by Someone as more than what the very rich gave—simply because it was all she had to give, a sacrifice. It was called the "widow's mite." It was a powerful remembrance to be recorded into the annals of time. That which had been tried in solitude broke into evidence in the public. It was in this area of faith and courage that she was above her fellows. What was so special and different about the widow's mite?

There was a very popular song in the sixties titled, "Just Ask the Lonely," and as I was thinking about it, I remembered part of the lyrics:

> When you feel that you can make it all alone.
> Remember no one is big enough to go it alone.
> Just ask the lonely.
> They know the hurt and pain
> Of losing a love you can never regain.

> — The Four Tops. Ask the Lonely

A love you can never regain . . .

There are some that have been in relationships of which there was never a marriage, and for some reason, there was a separation—a dissolvement of the relationship which was more painful than was anticipated. It was a death of a relationship because it could not be reconciled.

In either case, living or through death, it is a snatching away of someone out of your life, and no matter how many years that you spent together, you are left with a void that no one seems to understand but you. It is coupled with a loneliness that is like a deep, dark bottomless pit.

You have lost your lover, friend, and constant companion who was a tremendous and important part of your life. It was a relationship you had invested so much into.

I think about so many people that give all that they have and were many times left unappreciated and no longer recognized. Thus, the understanding of the widows, who are a special group of people. Widow: Defined as a person who has lost a spouse, creating a void in their life. I spoke to a widow one time soon after her husband's death, and she said she felt like a big empty bucket. He had filled her life so that she now felt drained of everything.

Understandably, this person had been there for a very long time. They had found their soul mate and formed a special connection that they had with no one else. They had gone through the years of marriage that it took to learn one another, resulting in two individuals becoming one and settling in to enjoy the years of marriage afforded them, and that was now over. Some became widows very young, losing that loved one after just a few years of marriage. It's still a love you can never regain.

The Widow's Mite

Marriage itself requires *sacrifice,* as any relationship that was a commitment for any length of time. You gave all that you had in a relationship with a person, now only to feel an emptiness that is comparable to none. Loneliness is a word that really cannot adequately describe your day-to-day emotions. You now sit in a car alone, go to those places that you used to frequent with them, alone. Memories flood your heart as you see other couples, even holding hands; you experience a stab of pain in your heart. Will it ever be the same again? Will it ever get better? You feel that you are just a very small person in a crowd, yet separated from all because of this status. Nights are the very worst.

How do you see yourself? How does God, who allowed this, see you? This, indeed, is a great *sacrificial offering* given from your very life.

Widowhood or any broken relationship that cannot be restored is where you find yourself left alone with some great (and to be truthful— some not-so-fond) memories. But it is something about a separation and dissolving of a relationship that you sacrificed and put so much into that is indescribable. As time goes by, you tend to remember the good times more, and that will overshadow the bad times. It makes you long for what *was* or what *could have been.*

I picture that widow going into the synagogue, giving all that she had, and leaving with an emptiness, not recognized by others because those that are recognized are those that give the most numerically. The sense is "after I have done my best, what is left for me? ..."

Emptiness. Missing that person. There is now a void, a darkness, and anxiety can follow with the question: "Will this space ever be filled again?" How often this leads to depression.

Anxiety and depression are on the rise, and they begin a vicious cycle. Often loneliness is the contributing factor.

A statistic report says nearly half of American adults report feeling lonely and left out some or most of the time. Another statistic revealed a slightly lower number reported that they feel isolated from others. [1]

The feeling of abandonment is not ever good because *"it is not good for the man [/woman] to be alone"* (Gen. 2:18).

Anything that is abandoned is neglected, and to be neglected too long (as in the case of a house, car, or other things) results in deterioration. So can it be for a person.

To be honest, many days, we might be those people— the desperate, the hurting, the lonely—just needing someone to notice, to slow down, to take time, to care.

Good news! Jesus did—seeing the real size of a widow's gift, and most important, her heart—as she dropped two coins into a temple collection box. He described what it meant for her as He said, "This poor widow has put more into the treasury than all the others," (Mark 12:43) because she gave her all, a sacrifice!

---

[1]   Health insurer Cigna's 2018 U.S. Loneliness Index. https://www.usnews.com/news/health-care-news/articles/2018-05-01/study-many-americans-report-feeling-lonely-younger-generations-more-so

Our *emotions*. For we don't like to use the word *depression* when we describe our feelings, but there are many words that have the same definition: "downcast," "brokenhearted," "troubled," "miserable," "despairing," "mourning," among others. Throughout the Bible are a number of stories about godly, influential men and women of faith who struggled and battled through dark times of hopelessness and depression. Many of us may find ourselves struggling there today.

Let's Turn the Corner to More Good News

We don't have to stay and be stuck there. There's hope. The widow was by herself but not alone. The One that knows the infinite knowledge of her life is there.

As Hagar, the young lady recorded in Genesis, found when she ran from her persecutor, maybe is what we need to remember still today. Her words breathed out this great truth that secures our struggles and anchors our hope: "You are the God who sees me" (Gen. 16:13) — El Roi.

El Roi – He is the God who *sees*: notices, looks at intently, has regard for, observes, considers, watches over, gives attention to, gazes upon, who keeps on seeing. That's our God. That's the One who created us. That's the One who loves so greatly and chases after us with good.

Don't ever think for a minute He doesn't see you, or care. You are not invisible to Him. Your situation is never too desperate for Him to work a miracle. He saw then; He sees now, every moment in the lives of His children. And He works, constantly works on our behalf, sometimes even sending an angel. Ask Hagar. (See Genesis 16.) You are never alone. He chased after Hagar in the desert; He knows where we are in our wilderness too.

As we remember this widow that came to the temple to give what she had, we realize how she also was noticed by "the God who sees." The Someone who noticed her saw her as being more important than all the others that gathered with their robes of authority, expensive clothing, and jewelry, and who were recognized by all that were there because of the important positions they held.

That person was Jesus: Lord of all, mender of broken hearts, abundant life giver. He not only *saw* her, but he *knew* her. She kept quiet about her situation, but He recognized what others considered a tiny donation was a sacrifice for her. He sees our lives the same way— the sacrifices we have made. "Touched with the feelings of [her] infirmities" (Heb. 4:13 KJV), He recognized this widow for who she really was. Though she didn't have much materially, He knew her worth even much more than she did. Because your worth is not determined by your assets or relationships as others determined, you can find comfort in His limitless understanding.

Jesus saw her, not as the others—the others who defined giving as a sign for what they had accomplished and thereby displayed it proudly. He saw her and made the astounding statement to all those assembled that she had given more than all those that were there. You see, again, He saw her heart. Even with its brokenness, void, and hurts. Yet she did not withdraw but was willing to give to others. He sees your heart. He knows you better than anyone.

What Do You Do with A Broken Heart?

Historically widows, in that day, were the least of all. When your spouse died, your support and so much more were lost, and you inevitably stood alone. There was no social security, widow's pension, or insurance plan. Unless you had children who contributed to your needs (though they had responsibilities of their own), you were really all alone. Yet this widow dared to step out and give out of her needs to what she felt was more important. We don't know her motivation except it was placed in the right place. There was always someone less fortunate than she, who chose not to have a pity party because of her loneliness and the vast vacancies that her life was now exhibiting. Rather she made a choice to look on the things of others more than herself. (See Phil. 2:3-4.)

She knew what was most important than anything else and chose not to put the little that she had in in a savings account, or tuck it away for a rainy day, or hold on to it until times got better. With such sacrifice, the Lord is well pleased, and He acknowledged. **Willingness is all God asks of us** — willingness to lay a little of what we have in His hands and watch Him transform it into something beautiful. The amount of the gift doesn't matter. Just like the widow with only a mite in Mark Chapter 14, we may be scraping the bottom of our purses to give. And when we come up with the little we have left and humbly offer it to God, He does with it exactly what Jesus did with the little boy's five loaves and two fish. He multiplies our little beyond our comprehension. (See John 6:9-13.)

What did the widow and the little boy have in common that made their giving so dear and pleasing to God? The answer is their hearts. They had the same willing heart behind their generosity. We serve a God of abundance who cares more about the heart of the giver than the gift itself.

A person that sacrifices, looking to help others and not thinking of themselves in their loneliness, learns an important truth. They learn and experience the blessings and the benefits that come out of it is a promise given. It is a promise so important at a time in your life when you tend to withdraw into a dark place feeling sorry for yourself. The only party you have is your pity party. You place an elaborate lace cloth on a table of memories, put out the best china representing the past great times, serve the tea of loneliness (with 2 teaspoons of heartbreak) and have the best "pity party ever!" You invite only those that will join in and have it with you. Your thoughts are only of yourself— *understandable but not excusable.*

Grief is a necessary process because we should grieve
.... but not without hope.

Many times, we are looking over our shoulders at our own experiences and grieve. We grieve over loss, disappointments, dreams that may have died. God challenges us to no longer grieve over the past but hold on to the promises that He always restores things better than they were, though we may not see it now. It will be in His timing. *His timing.*

Grieving will keep us from pressing into our new season. Grief manifests strongly, which can cause us to experience loss of vision. Consider the Bible example of Samuel grieving over King Saul. (See 1 Sam. 16.) Samuel cried about what had become of a great plan but resulted in the failure of Israel's first King. God had chosen Saul as the first King of Israel and sent Samuel, the prophet, to anoint him for that purpose. (See 1 Sam. 9-10.) The potential, success, and greatness that *could* have been died as he made choices that ended up with him being forsaken by God and his resulting death.

God had to speak to Samuel to get up from that place of grief. It was important for Samuel to shift out of his grief so that he could continue and fulfill his destiny. There were greater things that God had in store for him and was requiring of him. He had to leave the past in the past in order to move forward. He had to stop thinking about himself although the situation had affected him; there was a greater work that was being required of him. Destiny awaits ...

There is life after the loss. There is more adventure waiting for you, but it will be seen as you travel on the path of sacrifice, doing for others and thinking about someone other than yourself. Notice the widow after her giving. Jesus did not send his disciples running after her to give her a bag of money. Why? because He knows the benefits and the blessings that come with giving— sacrificial giving.

They all gave out of their wealth; but she, out of her poverty, put in everything she had to live on —Mark 12:44

Sacrificial giving… Strange formula for moving forward. Strange for healing a broken heart and filling a void? You will learn: His ways are not our ways, and His thoughts are not ours. (See Isa. 55:8.) In so doing, you will see that heart that was broken will start mending as your focus changes. The blessings will follow as goodness and mercy follow you—all the days of your life. (See Ps. 23:6.)

Let's take a journey with another widow and see how the reality of this truth played out for her, and the lessons we can learn. Oh, and how she was blessed beyond measure—*losing a love and finding another.*

Table of Contents

Chapter 1

Separation and Loss Have No Age Limit

—⟨⟩⟨⟩—

This brings us to the introduction of a woman named Ruth. She met her husband in the land of Moab, which was her home. He was not from there but was a transient from Bethlehem, the land of God's people, the Israelites. The Lord God Jehovah was their God and had made many promises to them.

Bethlehem actually means "bread." However, there came a famine in that land. Ruth's husband's father, Elimelech, chose to leave Bethlehem, take his family, and go to Moab for resources.

Moab was located just short of the Promised Land that Jehovah God had for His people. The Moabites were historically regarded as the perpetual enemy of the Israelites, «God›s Chosen People.» Physically, the region was a green, verdant valley in the middle of a serious desert. It was an "emerald in the sand," so to speak. Now you understand why this was the place that Elimelech chose to take his family, despite the inhabitants being enemies of the Israelites.

Desperate times will force us to take desperate measures. And often, decisions made then are not the best ones in those terrible times in our lives. I am sure the question came up: "If we are God's

chosen people, why is there a famine in *our* land while our enemies are living in a land that is the greenest, most fertile land, and
prospering?" So, it was understandable why Elimelech, who had a
family and wanted the best for them, went there. However, it is so
much like us not to stand and work through problems and to run
when things get tough, seeking better opportunities. The grass is
greener on the other side ... but when you get there, what do you
find? Know that not every open door is the open door for *you* and
that a better life is behind it.

Elimelech made the decision for his family—not the best—but
it was the providence of God for Ruth. Even in the worst decisions,
it can be working together for the good of someone. It was for Ruth
and her destiny.

Ruth is an example of how God can take a devastation in a life,
change that life, and take it in a direction *He* has foreordained. We
can see God working out His perfect plan in Ruth's life, just as He
does with all His children. Although she came from a pagan background in Moab, once she met the God of Israel, Ruth became a
living testimony to Him by faith. But I'm getting ahead of my story.
Ruth is not, of course, a widow at this time.

Back to the story. Elimelech took his wife, Naomi, and their
two sons, Mahlon and Chilion, and journeyed to Moab when the
famine came to Bethlehem. The sons married, choosing wives from
the women of Moab. I can imagine when that son, Mahlon, saw
Ruth— this beautiful Moabite woman with suntanned or geneti-
cally brown beautiful skin and with long, beautiful thick hair—he
did not care about her heritage or lineage. He just wanted to make
her his wife, and he did. It is not recorded exactly how long their
marriage was; however, it was about ten years tracing this history.
We know he died, along with his brother; and Ruth became a widow.

What a change in her life that was certainly not anticipated! She had enjoyed the comfort of a home that was built on principles of godliness with a man that chose to love and cherish "til death do us part." I can only imagine the thoughts that ran through her head: "I had finally met a man, like no other, certainly not like the men of Moab. A man who served the God who, Himself, has designed marriage, thereby also giving the directions for a good marriage. We followed those directions, and our marriage was great because of it. We were looking forward to having children and a long, happy life together."

Her dreams had come to pass, a realization of what happiness really is. But death came to claim and end all her future hopes and dreams before they could be fully realized— and so soon. Death is not willingly anticipated, but it is a reality in life.

Love lost, love snatched from you unwillingly, leaving your heart empty and void. There is a feeling that you will never be loved or be capable of loving again—suddenly. What did Alfred Lord Tennyson, say? "'Tis better to have loved and lost than never to have loved at all"?

Author's Note: My thought was, *Sorry, those words are of no comfort. Did he really love anyone and lose that love?* But research on the matter revealed that he penned those words after the sudden death of a dear friend. (See his poem, "In Memoriam A. H. H.")

I am not feeling this because right now, the loss is greater than the love experienced. If I had not experienced this love, I would not hurt so badly. "Love ended, life seems not too far behind," my emotions are saying. I know it is emotions, but they are just as real right now. These are the sentiments, sorrows and anguish of love lost.

But a lost love can be the beginning of a greater future, though you don't realize it at the time

Even as a widow, Ruth's *purpose* had not ended. She would realize when one journey ends, destiny does not. **Now that's great news!**

When a relationship ends, life is not over. We can move forward and see a new beginning. God is not through with us yet. It's the decisions we make at this time in our lives that are most important.

Ruth's loss was a husband, but in looking at Naomi, we see her loss is unprecedented. She loses her husband and both sons. Plus, she is in a foreign land with no one to turn to in her tremendous grief.

Naomi decides to go back home to Bethlehem where her people are. Leaving this place that she had tried to make home, with all the unfamiliar surroundings, and going to a place of familiarity where people loved her was a comfort in itself. Her two daughters-in-law follow her. Why would they leave the familiarity of their homeland to go to an entirely unfamiliar environment? This is not understandable but could be answered by the Jewish traditions.

Jewish traditions say that if a man dies, the brother has to marry the dead brother's widow and raise up children through her so that the family name will continue. So dutifully, the sisters-in-law either follow Naomi from tradition, or what other alternative do they have? It's either a faith walk or just a duty, for there's no other solution that I can see for the moment because I find myself in a valley of indecision. This valley is walled by my grief, loss, and hurts that have surrounded me and have the potential to consume me. I just move and walk with perhaps others that are walking in that direction at this time in my life.

What is your walk at this time?

Are you believing that God has a greater plan for you? Are you willing to leave the familiar comfort zone, or are you just moving to be moving in the usual direction, but with no hope or insight? This brings us to the difference between Ruth and Orpah (Naomi's other daughter-in-law). *Which one are you?*

Orpah just moved with tradition, or respect, or perhaps out of loneliness, with no place to go but with Naomi, though her heart was really back in the past—in Moab. You can never move forward with your heart or even one foot in the past. It takes two feet to move forward. Take the time to jump right now out of the past…come on, I'm waiting.… *Jump*! Put your faith to work physically. *Jump*! Notice it takes two feet? *Jump*! You just left everything behind you, although it may be close (depending on how far you can jump) but you made a first move.

As Ruth would learn, God had something greater and better for her, but she had to leave those things behind and press forward. That sounds a little like what the Apostle Paul said, "Forgetting those things which are behind . . . I press toward the mark . . . of the high calling." (Phil. 3:13-14 KJV).

Oh my, I'm getting ahead of my story again . . .

Naomi walks away from Moab with Ruth and Orpah at her side. In contemplation, she says to them, "Go, return each to [your] mother's house" (Ruth 1:8). She really thought this was best for them. There will always be someone that will give you advice to return to the memoires or the last place where you left them. They mean well, but this is not the place God has for you. However, if you are looking for some agreement, especially when you really don't want to go forward, this is a welcomed release.

Chapter 2

Making Decisions in the Crossroads of Life

Surely we will return with you to your people
(Ruth 1:10)

Politely, Ruth and Orpah both said to Naomi, "Surely we will return with you to your people" (Ruth 1:10). But Naomi encourages them to follow what they are feeling with the words, of the Jewish tradition. Allow me to paraphrase verse 11: "There are no more sons within me at my age that can be your husbands." What was Naomi saying? In the absence of an heir or son, Judaic laws permitted a Levirate marriage, which passed the deceased man's name and property to his son or the next available male relative. This heir had a responsibility to marry the widow and preserve the family name and heritage. The law said specifically: "And it shall be, that the firstborn which she beareth shall succeed in the name of his brother which is dead, that his name be not put out of Israel" (Deut. 25:6 KJV).

Naomi is saying (and again I paraphrase): "Would you really wait for them to be grown so that they can marry you? Do you really want to be a 'cougar extreme'?"

Orpah, thinks about this and says (in her heart; it's not recorded, but in my imagination, I can hear her say): "Now that is the truth! I'm going back to what I am comfortable with, what I am used to. My mama is there for me. She didn't want me to marry out of my class/family-type anyway. I remember Joab; I remember Balak. I'm going back!" Those memories of the past are stronger than any hope for the future. She kisses Naomi bids her farewell and returns to Moab. Her choice for her future was the past—and God honors that.

But here is the difference. Ruth, destiny minded, was not thinking just about herself. She remembers what she saw during the time in this family of God.

Things can only get better when you move forward. She really didn't understand or could see her future. But she saw what had been proven and what would work, even though she had experienced tragedy in her life: widowhood, separation, and a great void left from the one she loved.

She tells Naomi, "Entreat me not to leave you. . . . Wherever you go, I will go. . . . Your people shall be my people. . . . [Most importantly], Your God, my God" (Ruth 1:16). In essence, she was saying to her mother-in-law, "I will take this faith walk with you."

Rather than a spiritual "plateau," faith is actually a process that involves increasing degrees of trust throughout life. *Little faith* **hopes** that God will do what He says, *strong faith* **knows** that He will; and *great faith* **believes** that He has already done it. I want to see it the way God sees it. His thoughts of you are "for [good] and not of evil, to give you an expected end" (Jer. 29:11 KJV).

Many people will give you advice during this time of your life, some really good but not applicable to you. See what is really working. Ask where is there true success? Know what your destiny is. If you don't know, there is Someone who does. He knows you better than anyone else, even than you. David the psalmist said:

> O Lord, you have searched me and known me. You know my down sitting and my rising up. You understand my thought afar off. You comprehend my path and my lying down, and are acquainted with all my ways. For there is not a word on my tongue, but behold, O Lord, you know it altogether. You have hedged me behind and before, and laid your hand upon me. Such knowledge is too wonderful for me; It is high, I cannot attain it. Where can I go from your Spirit? Or where can I flee from your presence. —Ps.139:1-7

Does it not make sense to see what *He* has to say about your future? Wow, that is enough for me!

He will give you the grace to let go, to surrender all

Naomi and Ruth continue their journey forward to Bethlehem. Both widows, both in bereavement, but going to the right place. Ruth is willing to sacrifice everything for this entirely new adventure in serving her mother-in-law, not thinking about herself. (Her *widow's mite.*) It is always when you think about others, and you take your mind off of your immediate problems that you find out goodness and mercy will follow you. It is the widow's mite— all

11

that she has but is greater than any larger amount that anyone else can give, because it is given with her heart.

A kingdom principle is stewardship. My friend, Pastor Wayne Bass, says: "This puts you in direct partnership with God. This benefit is strategic (and somewhat ironic) since it relates to the fulfilling privilege of service, which takes place at the intersection of human brokenness and Divine Grace."

Ruth was stepping into the future but also stepping with a foundation under her. It was not blind faith because faith is not blind. She was taking a leap of faith. She jumped out of her past but now is walking in faith into her future. Naomi's God would be her God—the God of Abraham, Isaac, and Jacob; the God of promise; the God who had promised. She did not allow the wounds that had left scars of her past prevent her from moving forward.

The scars represent your past but do not dictate your future

They came to the threshold of Bethlehem. Bethlehem, remember, means "bread." Will it be the place that would feed them and supply all that they needed? Not just physically, but the emotional and spiritual needs that make a person whole. Will the "Love" that everyone needs, that we are created by and for be found there? **Love.** No life can thrive or is ever completed without love. There is no substitute, though many try to fill voids in their life with other things instead of love. We were made to be loved; in fact, our Creator *is* love. (See 1 John 4:8.) This love is to be experienced, and He wants us all to experience it. Would Bethlehem be that place?

Well jumping out of her past ... The women enter into the gate. All the city recognizing Naomi was excited at her arrival. Coming back to a good home is always a welcomed relief. It's not a step back but a place of stabilization to regroup, a place to refresh, to get your bearings, to continue in the direction of your destiny. Sometimes, God allows you to what appears like stepping back, but it's actually a place to re-direct because you have gotten off course. It doesn't always have to be a geographical place, but it's always the place where I come to myself and recognize my compass is off, and I need to change. Our heavenly Father is always there to direct; don't forget, He allowed it.

The women greet them saying, "Is this Naomi?" (Ruth 1:19). Now, Naomi's name means *my joy, my bliss,* or *pleasantness of Jehovah*....but Naomi quickly corrects them and says, "Call me Mara" (which means "bitter") and gives the reason: "For the Almighty has dealt very bitterly with me" (See v. 20.) Just because you know God and the place to return to does not mean that you don't have the residue of emotional scars and that they have not been dealt with. The pain and the hurt of your loss and the separation are still felt acutely; and when you don't understand why, it is easy to place blame wrongfully, with wrong motives when misunderstood. God did not change her name. She changed it in her hurt, and it led to her being bitter.

Naomi explains the reason for her pain. "I went out full, and the Almighty has brought me home again empty." When you nurture the pain and sometimes it is so intense that you can't see anything else but what Naomi says, "[The Lord] has testified against me and [He] has afflicted me." (See v. 21.) Oh, if only she knew that He has said, "For I know the plans I have for you . . . plans to prosper you and not to harm you, plans to give you hope and a future" (Jer. 29:11). You see, He allowed it for a great cause in your life, Naomi. Though you can't see it now, He sees much farther than you ever could. The reality is, sometimes, He may allow something that He detests for the greater good.

But, Naomi, you are home now where He will supply all of your needs and fill the void. Home is where the people of God are and where the presence of the Lord is found. And "in [His] presence is fullness of joy" (Ps. 16:11 KJV) and where His love is.

Look externally at this combination: two widows, empty, alone, no means of support, and seemingly no future. An older woman, who has tasted the cup of bitterness and feels her life is over. She feels as if God actually was talking against her and was doing nothing but afflicting her. A younger woman, who seems destined to take care of her, was her future.... But a great opportunity for The Lord God Almighty to work. Just ripe for a miracle. Sounds like a great foundation for a love story and the planting of seeds for a great harvest. Huh?

God's timing— always perfect, because it was the beginning of the barley harvest in Bethlehem.

Chapter 3

Settling Into a New Life's Season...
With Expectations

Naomi and Ruth get settled in. It's home for Naomi, and she has a relative on her husband's side named Boaz, so she is not completely without family relationship. However, this is a completely new environment for Ruth. Life starts in Bethlehem and responsibilities, along with provisions, are at the top of the list.

It was harvest time in Bethlehem, and Ruth, seeing a way to provide for them, asked Naomi if she would consent to letting her go into the fields and gather the fallen grain behind anyone who allowed her to (which was provisions for the poor).

Ruth did not go into her new home (as we can sometimes do) with a sense of entitlement just because she knew Naomi. We say, "It's not *what* you know; it's *who* you know, networking. Attach yourself to those that are in the know." Nor did Ruth go wallowing in grief looking for sympathy. She didn't go seeking grief counseling or the "New Widows' Support Group" (although there is certainly nothing wrong with doing that).

Here is the key as Ruth enters into this new season in her life as a servant: She is concerned about the needs of Naomi and willing to sacrifice for her more than herself. She is the epitome of humility as she even asks Naomi for *permission* to work in a field to provide for them. And not just working a field but to walk *behind* someone that drops what they gather—the leftovers of the harvest— *if* they allow her to do so. A truth is in motion—because "God resists the proud, but gives grace to the humble" (James 4:6). This touches the heart of God, of course, who will start opening doors for this woman not just with provisions for their needs, but destiny is being orchestrated.

> *Where are you in this journey? What decisions are you making in response to your pain?*

Take your widow's mite—what you have to give—and give to someone else in service, and you will experience the grace of our Lord and doors opening to serve. Walk through them, not for yourself but for someone else; and watch your life start turning in a direction that will not only surprise you but will allow you to experience the abundance: results of a sacrificial life.

God, who preserved His people, is upholding us today as well. He can help us in any environment. We may worry about enduring another season. But the Bible assures us that God, who cares so wonderfully for the lilies of the field that are here today and gone tomorrow, can also provide for our needs. (See Matthew 6:28-30.)

A widow's mite does not have to be money. Many use money to cover and negate the responsibility or opportunity that God is giving us to serve sacrificially. It's digging down into that part of you that makes it a sacrifice to do something that is not easy. We understand that there is a process to grief, but grief can make you self-absorbent. Offering your widow's mite makes you turn from your hurts, wounds, and pain forcing you to take your eyes off of yourself and do something for someone else. With that comes a healing you had no idea would come.

Accepting what God allows and receive what He sends

You see, God's ways are so far from ours; even His thoughts are so much higher than ours. This now becomes a time in our journey/season that we get opportunity to trust Him, even when we don't understand. Now can be a time of trusting what God allows at this time in our lives; for receiving the people that He sends to speak into our lives.

Ruth trusts Naomi's wisdom, submits to her authority, and goes into the field to "work"—no ulterior motives— but just to work. Ruth enters the field to gather grain behind the harvesters. It is another foreign place for her.

God always provides for His people. Here is what Leviticus 19:9 says:"When you [the owner] reap the harvest of your land, do not reap to the very edges of your field or gather the gleaming of your harvest. Do not go over your vineyard a second time or pick up the grapes that have fallen. Leave them for the poor and the foreigner. I am the Lord your God." Please note, these provisions were declared and made even before Naomi and Ruth were in need or were even born.

Ruth enters the field. Can you imagine? As she enters, eyes are fixed on her and there are questions."Who is she?" Or "Who does she think she is? What right does she have being here?" Much like the widow in the temple, moving past those that felt they belonged more than she, she presses past them to give her sacrifice.

Always remember that God is at work on the other side of our obstacles, arranging the details and bringing His plans to fruition—remembering but not lamenting what we have lost but celebrating what we have found no matter how different it is.

Ruth finds work and a new home in a completely different environment. This does not sound like anything to celebrate at this time, but "In everything give thanks; for it is the will of God ...." (1 Thes. 5:18).

Chapter 4

Destiny Starts to Unravel

Then she left, and went and gleaned in the field after the reapers—Ruth 2:3

—⟨⟩⟨⟩—

Ruth worked and worked hard. Why is it that sometimes we feel purpose, destiny, or what is for us will just drop into our laps? Our journey will include a work ethic, and it's not all about us. Ruth worked to provide and give her widow's mite to someone else and will receive from someone, something far greater than she could ever imagine.

We are supposed to live on purpose, not just trying to exist each day. She worked with purpose but not for herself. God still has purpose for your life, although it appears that there is now none or that, that which you thought was purpose has been taken away.

Naomi told Ruth about a relative on her husband Elimelech's side, whose name was Boaz. Ruth asked her mother-in-law's permission to work in his fields to glean, and perhaps she would find grace. Naomi said, "Go, my daughter" (Ruth 2:2).

Grace— that unmerited favor given by God—something we don't deserve, but because of His love for us, He freely gives it. We can find it in the most unlikely places. Grace that is sustaining and sufficient we will learn in our journey in life.

Is it no wonder that Ruth ended up on Boaz's side of the field gleaning? Boaz had come from Bethlehem that day. He is found to be a cautious and gentle man who did not think highly of himself even though he was wealthy and prestigious. To me, this is seen and heard in his greetings to the reapers, the workers in his field: "The Lord be with you!" he says (v. 4). It's a simple greeting but so power packed. If the Lord is with you, there is no lack; if the Lord is with you, His face shines upon you and gives you peace. (See Num. 6:24-26.) *The Lord is my Shepherd; I shall not want. . . .*

Perhaps at this time for Boaz, there was a need, a void, a loneliness he was experiencing in his life that needed filling. Is his destiny unfolding also?

After Boaz's greeting to the reapers, they immediately replied, "The Lord bless you!" Though it was a traditional reply in response to his, it was providence. What appears sometimes as a coincidence is really providence. At that moment, he looks and sees Ruth. He says to the supervisor, who was over the reapers, "Whose young woman is this?" (v. 5).

She was not looking, busy in what she was tasked to do, but he saw her. From the woman's perspective, it is much to be said about how you are to be found—without looking yourself. In this day of web searchers on give-me-what-I-want.com, it is quite foreign not to in-depth search when so many avenues are made available to us. Maya Angelou once said, "A woman's heart should be so hidden in God that a man [her husband] has to seek Him just to find her."

Trusting the God of the Bible that says, "He who finds a wife finds a good thing, and obtains favor from the Lord" (Prov. 18:22) confirms God's declaration that will never fail, when we serve a God that never fails. Searching has its place, and it's a wise person that searches out a matter, but in decisions pertaining to life's matters and exactly what my future and potential is, I want to trust Him for those decisions. He is the One that knows me better than I know myself and all my tomorrows that I don't have a clue about. In fact, as far as the future is concerned, He has already been there. I don't search. I have learned to seek Him and allow him to take care of those things.

My husband passed and went to be with the Lord after our 47 years of marriage. As a widow, I am writing this. Forty-seven years prior to that, it was *a love found*. He found me sitting at a table in Moody Bible Institute's cafeteria. Here a love story begins.

I was trying to complete a paper that was due during the next class period. He saw me and introduced himself, as I tried to ignore him because of the short time that I had left, reading my text book and researching my Bible. He pursued me, got confirmation from the Lord we both served, and he declared that I would be his wife a very short time after our initial meeting.

What was I doing? Just what I was supposed to be doing at that time—preparing for what I was called to do, working—and God honored His Word by allowing Herbert Jason Russell to "find me." After 5 children, 18 grandchildren, and now 5 great grandchildren, does it work? Absolutely! I did not know what the future would hold, but God did, and He knew who I needed as a companion. My husband complemented me in every area of my life's purpose, and I also his.

While pastoring a church with multiple ministries for 36 years of our marriage, he encouraged my purpose and my destiny that were drawn up from the blueprint of my life by the Architect of my soul. What is so amazing is this was in the plans before I was just a twinkle in my daddy's eye, before my mother even found out she was pregnant. There is a word in Hebrew called *brecha*, which means "my soul mate," and my husband definitely was that as my greatest supporter and cheerleader. Now, this is a real love story because it was God's love that orchestrated it. I have learned to obey the Word of God, which I have found is trustworthy, and watch Him fulfill the promises He has for me. In our marriage, many times it was *iron sharpening iron* (See Prov. 27:17) as God used it to make us *individually* and become *one* with purpose.

How many promises have been made to you, only to be broken as easily as made? Some were intentional, some unintentional. A promise is only valuable as the one making it has trustworthy character and the ability to carry through. Our heavenly Father is truthful, faithful, loving, and all powerful. We can base our entire life on His promises, secure in the knowledge that He will do just as He has said and what His Word declares. Herbert found me and found favor with God.

Back to our story.... Well, Boaz sees Ruth. Who is this woman that stands out from all the rest? Her beauty is seen, but it is not the outward beauty that is the instant attraction. He enquires about her. The reapers tell him she is the young Moabite woman who came back with Naomi from the country of Moab.

Now, if written on paper, Boaz's bio would describe him as a man of great power, wealth, and influence. Therefore, a connection with Ruth, a widow, a foreigner with nothing, would have been almost impossible.

I can imagine the scene: Ruth hears the sound of the hoofs of a horse and feels his presence without looking up. She slowly raises her head, looks, and sees this overpowering man of strength with eyes that seemingly pierce her very soul. She is at first speechless but then tells Boaz her simple request: to glean and gather among the sheaves after the reapers.

Her work ethic is impeccable, expecting no favors. She works from early morning until evening, with just a short rest. This, unknown to Ruth, was a witness of her character and tenacity. She was granted a task that she requested, which to help someone else. Again, a widow's mite, a sacrifice of all that she had to give, but recognized by someone meaningful.

Boaz speaks to Ruth, giving her advice: "Listen, my daughter [a term of endearment and protection].... Do not go to glean in another field, nor go from here, but stay close by my young women" (Ruth 2:8).

Don't ever lose the connection whereby God has placed you. The grass always looks greener on the other side, in the other field. Bloom where you have been planted, and the fragrance that God has given you (no one else has it) will draw those that are destined to be a part of your life.

Boaz's further instruction was to "Let your eyes be on the field which they reap, and go after them" (v. 9). *Ruth, don't look any further.* (Because what she needed was right there.) One of the enemy's tools is to get you to take your focus off of your purpose and look to see what you might think to be other opportunities. But not every open door is a door that you are destined to go through to fulfill your purpose.

*Don't allow yourself to get stuck doing meaningful, but
not purpose-driven things*

Are you one of those people who dives into every exciting idea, thinking, "If it's a good thing, why not? I have found (and it took me so long to learn) it's an exhausting way to live. The better way is to know your purpose and pursue *it*. There is another promise in the Bible that says it better. "Seek first the kingdom of God and His righteousness (He knows your purpose), and all these things shall be added to you" (Matt. 6:33). There is no peace or safety except in the perfect will of God for your life. Providence, purpose, and destiny are found when a person's steps are ordered by the Lord, and we will also see protection as we continue to look at Ruth's story.

Boaz says to Ruth these words: "Have I not commanded the young men not to bother you?" (v.9). Not only does he supply protection but also provision. He continues, "And when you are thirsty, go to the vessels and drink from what the young men have drawn" (v. 9). This widow's mite of sacrifice is beginning to symbolize a seed planted into her destiny and is now beginning to reap a great harvest in her life.

Just as Jesus recognized that widow that share her mite, Boaz is recognizing what a wonderful woman Ruth is. She was not carrying any credentials that stated her worthiness of entitlement, but it was her character that preceded her, without her even knowing. For she is totally surprised that he has noticed her and is showing her favor. She, a foreigner, that has no rights or entitlements.

Let her own works praise her in the gates—Prov. 31:31

Boaz tells Ruth he has heard about how she has taken care of her mother-in-law after she became a widow and how she sacrificially left her own mother and father and her homeland to come there with her. On this journey in life, there are so many times when you feel you are not seen or appreciated for all that you do, but you just continue. Someone that really counts sees you and your unselfish labor of love. With every act of love, you are planting seeds for your harvest. You will reap what you sow is an undeniable principle that has existed and operated since the beginning of time itself. So be careful of the seeds you sow. (See Gal. 6:7.)

Boaz now speaks a blessing upon Ruth: "The Lord repay your work, and a full reward be given you by the Lord God of Israel, under whose wings you have come for refuge" (v. 12). Though God's methodology is to use people to speak into our lives and help us on this journey, we should always recognize it does not matter who gets the credit, as long as God gets the glory. Notice, Boaz does not say "I," but "The Lord" repay you. The Lord would use Boaz.

What else had Boaz seen in Ruth? An important truth. He acknowledged that Ruth had learned to trust God. Her trust was not in Naomi (who was giving her great advice) nor the link with being related to Boaz and coming to the field to network. Her trust was not in the amount that she would receive from working, nor the man that she met. She came to know and trust the living God, and He would meet all of her needs and use whoever He wanted to.

Oh, that men would praise the Lord for his goodness, and for his wonderful works to the children of men!

For He satisfieth the longing soul and fills the hungry soul with goodness. —Ps. 107:8-9 KJV

Ruth, though she trusted God, had an attitude of gratitude! How can you not thank the people that God uses to bless you? She thanks Boaz for what he is doing and finds favor in his sight. The power of praise and being thankful opens even more doors for you. With this comment from Ruth, Boaz gives her an invitation that at lunch time she should come eat with him and his reapers. (See v. 14.) Prior to this, remember, she was beneath the reapers, just gathering what was left over. She ate sufficiently—nothing more, nothing less. But by the time she left for the fields again, Boaz told the reapers not to be rude to her, to let her glean among the sheaves (not the left overs, but the harvest itself) and even to pull out some bunches for her on purpose! (See vv. 15-16.) Destiny is unfolding, step-by-step and each step a miracle.

I believe another key to her success during this time was simply *moving forward*. Leaving those things that are behind, not wallowing in self-pity (whose twin sister is Self-centered). "It really is all about me now. There is no one else in my world that is hurting like me. Everyone needs to migrate to me as a nucleus, the center of attention, and help *me*. There is no life outside of my grief." But it is; so, look for the light that will be provided and walk therein, forward.

I'm not negating memories because good memories are to be reflected on. Recalling the good times you had can be refreshing and bring smiles to your face, remembering the way we *were*. But you cannot allow them to hold you hostage to the past, whereby they prevent you from moving forward. *A museum is a great place to visit but not to live.*

Ruth is given opportunity to move forward; and she does— each step, going through each door as they are opened for her. Through each door is a pleasant surprise as her destiny starts unfolding, step-by-step. Not all at once, but step-by-step, and each step is purpose-driven, not for herself but for someone else. She finds goodness, mercy, grace, and favor are following her.

Ruth gathers until evening; then thrashes the barley she has gathered which amounts to about an ephah (a little over a bushel). She returns to town, and Naomi sees how much she has gathered. Ruth also "brought out and gave to her what she had kept back after she had been satisfied [after eating lunch with Boaz and his reapers]" (v. 18). Note, she did not store up for herself; she was always willing to share. Her mother-in-law is surprised and asked her, "Where have you gleaned today? And where did you work? Blessed be the one who took notice of you" (v. 19). Naomi recognizes that it was someone else that had intervened for her to reap a blessing such as that, and she takes the time to bless him and speak well of Him.

A Praise Pause

> *Never be so future-focused that you don't take the time to celebrate **your now**!*

No matter how dire a circumstance is or what situation you find yourself in, there will always be something that you can be thankful for. And when the problems pile up and seemingly have no end, that's when it's the most difficult to be grateful. It's also the time when we need to show gratitude the most.

When that time comes, take time to be thankful, no matter how small it may appear. You will always find your blessings will far exceed your complaints. Whatever it is—take time to say thank you. Never have a sense of entitlement. You will find having an attitude of gratitude will open other doors for you. Praise God from whom all blessings flow; also take time to thank those vehicles that the blessings came through. God still uses people.

Ruth tells Naomi about the one at whose place she had been working. "The name of the man I worked with today is Boaz" (v.19). Naomi again asks the Lord's blessings on him for his good deeds and recognizes who the blessings come from. "He has not stopped showing his kindness to the living and the dead. . . . That man is our close relative; he is one of our guardian-redeemers" (v. 20).

What is a *guardian-redeemer* or *kinsman-redeemer* as it is referred to in some other Bible translations? Stick with me; more on that later. All still in God's plan for Ruth's life.

Was it a coincidence? Not at all. What catches us by surprise has been predestined for us. Even when we go in another direction, and our life becomes all snarled up, we need to offer it to our Lord, and let Him untie the knots. You will see; God will show His grace and mercy.

As if a light seems to come on at that moment, Ruth goes on to tell her mother-in-law how Boaz even said to stay with the workers until they finish harvesting all his grain. Naomi confirms the wisdom that was spoken to her from Boaz saying, "Go with the women who work for him, because in someone else's field you might be harmed" (v. 22). Always, "in the multitude of counselors there is safety" (Prov. 11:14). Purpose is established by counsel. (See Prov. 20:18.)

Heed spoken wisdom because it is so easy to start striking out on your own, feeling you can handle it. Take a lesson from sheep. Sheep that stay in the fold with the shepherd and other sheep are doubly protected. It's when the wolf lures a solitary sheep from out of the fold that, that sheep can be easily attacked and destroyed because there is no one there to defend him.

When you have been hurt, you are particularly vulnerable, and you desire isolation. You will tend to not want to be around others, building walls and not allowing anyone to get close to you. The good news is we are created for relationship. Therefore, it is not good for a man/woman to be alone. Just because one relationship was terminated (for whatever reason), it does not mean God does not want you to have another or that He cannot provide you with another. Take down those walls of hurt. Allow the scar tissue of disappointment to be removed from your heart. Get ready to love again.

Ruth takes the wise council and stays close to the women of Boaz to glean until the barley and wheat harvest were finished, still living with her mother-in-law.

Chapter 5

When It Is Time to Step Out or Through the Next Door

> There is a time for everything,
> and a season for every activity under the heavens:
> A time to be born and a time to die
> A time to plant and a time to uproot,
> A time to kill and a time to heal
> A time to tear down and a time to build.
>
> —Eccl. 3:1-3

"One day Ruth's mother-in-law Naomi said to her, 'My daughter, I must find a home for you, where you will be well provided for'" (Ruth 3:1). It was time for Ruth to build her own home. Naomi goes on to say, "Now Boaz, with whose women you have worked, is a relative of ours" (v. 2).

*It is time to step away from them to go through
the next door*

How? Via the guardian-redeemer or kinsman-redeemer,
which Boaz was.

What was a guardian-redeemer? A "relative," which is the word
central to the narrative and message of the book of Ruth. Our
language has no equivalent, as the concept is related to the cultural obligation of a family member whose kinfolk has suffered
lost. It involved the capacity of the relative who may be qualified
to "redeem" another relative from slave status or recoup property
once owned but now lost by reason of indebtedness. The expression "kinsman-redeemer" (KJV) is often used for "relative," seeking
in English to convey the combination of a human relationship with
a divinely appointed role of "Recoverer."

God's provision for this day in Ruth's life was written as a
law almost 100 years before. What's more amazing is Ruth was a
Gentile widow who grew up outside of the Jewish faith and later
became the great-grandmother of King David... *Sorry, I'm getting
ahead of my story again.*

But you really get my point. Before you were formed in your
mother's womb, and even when you were out of the will of God..
.. You went through the pains and sufferings of life. You, however,
experienced the grace of God—that unmerited favor. He made
provisions for you that were exceedingly abundantly above all that
you could ever ask or think. (See Eph. 3:20.) *A divinely appointed
role of a recoverer just for you ... as was provided for Ruth.*

**There is a process with preparation. Not all at once
but step-by- step.**

After Naomi declares the relationship they have with Boaz, she continues her instruction to her daughter-in-law: "Tonight he will be winnowing barley on the threshing floor. [This was a process after the gathering it from the fields.] Wash, put on perfume, and get dressed in your best clothes. Then go down to the threshing floor, but don't let him know you are there until he has finished eating and drinking. When he lies down, note the place where he is lying. Then go and uncover his feet and lie down. He will tell you what to do" (Ruth 3:2-4). Yes, this was a custom—not a seduction. There is a difference.

Ruth's response, because of her trust in Naomi, was "I will do whatever you say" (v. 5). Was this unfamiliar custom difficult for her because she was not at all accustomed to their ways? It does not say, but I think she was. However, when you understand your purpose, you are willing to sacrifice, prepare, and go through the process. You trust the God who will lead and guide you, even when you don't understand. His ways and thoughts are not your thoughts. In fact, it is recorded in Isaiah 55:9: "For as the heavens are higher than the earth, so are My ways higher than your ways, and My thoughts than your thoughts." You have to trust Him as well as the process as you prepare for your destiny.

Can you imagine Ruth's emotions at this time? Trembling, as she obeys the wisdom of Naomi and lies down quietly, uncovering his feet. It was in the middle of the night. Boaz was startled; he turned —and there was a woman lying at his feet!

"Who are you? he asked."

"I am your servant, Ruth..." (v. 9).

*Well, I think I would have had problems with that instruction— **to lie at his feet**. Feet! what's wrong with **beside** him? I know it's your custom, but I'm not*

*lying at no man's feet. And **servant**! Are you kidding?
I'm not a slave for **no-bod-dy**!*

Let me continue on before I lose most of you. . . .

Ruth's answer tells you her attitude and an admirable char-
acteristic: "I am your servant, Ruth. . . . Spread the corner of your
garment over me, since you are a guardian-redeemer of my family"
(Ruth 3:9). By asking Boaz to take her under his wing, Ruth sought
to enter into the first stage of marriage betrothal. Purpose, not
seduction; obedience, not rebellion; humility, not prideful. *How do
we know? Listen to Boaz's answer:*

"The Lord bless you, my daughter. . . . This kindness is greater
than you showed earlier. [He continues to speak of her good character that has been displayed from the very beginning, which drew
him to notice her.] You have not run after the younger men, whether
rich or poor" (v. 10).

The wonderful lesson here: When you have an intimate devo-
tional life with Christ and are controlled by His Spirit, your life will
produce the fruit of His Spirit—love, joy, peace, patience, kindness,
goodness, faithfulness, gentleness, and self-control. (See Gal. 5:22-
23.) What man doesn't want to chase after a woman who is truly
joyful, peaceful, patient, kind, good, faithful, gentle, and—I believe
this one stands out among the others—self-controlled!

Now, Boaz says after her request, "I will do for you all you ask.
[There will be no problem because] all the people of my town know
that you are of noble character" (v. 11). Do you see the thread that
runs through this entire scene? Her character, reputation had gone
before her so that she did not have to speak for herself. They spoke
loudly, without her ever saying a word. We are living epistles read
of all men. (See 2 Cor. 3:1-5.) Let others read your life—not your
resume' or designer clothes, make-up, profession, popularity. . . .

A detour on the road on the way to destiny. (Ruth 3:12)

In traveling through the process, the road can take a sharp turn not planned, a detour where it might appear that you are going in reverse instead of forward. It is where at the road you are on that all of a sudden, you come to a road block! Yes, the end of this road. You can't go any further because there is a very large, plain sign that says **Detour**. How exasperating this can be. You were almost there, you thought. You had done all that was required of you, following the directions that were given you by the GPS (**G**od's **P**athway to **S**uccess). Sometimes, most times, however; nowhere in the directions did you get this warning or it said this was going to happen.

You are in the valley of decisions: Either quit; go back, it's not worth it. Or continue to follow the unplanned (unplanned for you) new directions. A sacrifice of more time, more waiting. Even in this, there is purpose in the wait. It's part of the process. Of course, you don't want to hear that now. Well, what is He saying about it? It's now time to stop, read the instructions, seek the Instructor. He certainly has not brought you this far to leave you.

Here is Ruth's glitch in her journey. I now call it a glitch because what can seem like a major detour with a vast waste of time in God's purpose for you is just a glitch, a hiccup on your way to your destiny. Pause to see what the "Author and finisher of your faith" has to say about it. (See Heb. 12:2.) What does the kinsman-redeemer say about it? You will find the glitch comes with a reason and instructions.

Did I tell you Boaz's name means "strength"? Isn't that interesting at this time?

*The Lord is my light and my salvation; Whom shall
I fear? The Lord is the strength of my life: Of whom
shall I be afraid?*

— Ps. 27:1

Here come the facts and the instructions. Boaz speaks, "It is true that I am a close relative; however, there is a relative that is closer than I" (Ruth 3:12). Before she can be in despair, he gives her this assurance: "If he will perform the duty of a close relative for you—good; let him do it. But if he does not want to perform the duty for you, then I will perform the duty for you, as the Lord lives!" (v. 13). [It's a win-win situation for you]. Oh my, the promise is signed, sealed, and delivered because my kinsman-redeemer lives!

Boaz had preceded his last remark to Ruth by telling her to wait there until the morning. Another wait? As the sun rises, trading places with the moon, a new time begins for her. But this time is with great expectation. Ruth could have thought and said, "Why waste my time waiting on Boaz? I'm going to find *the other* one." But her wait was for God's perfect will, which is not the *second* best. I wait for the best that God has for me. And *He* will work it out—not me. Sometimes we are tempted to run ahead and take that first offer, and we end up settling for less than God's best. Wait, and be of good courage.

So many are waiting—not waiting for just anyone, just any type of relationship resulting from loneliness, but waiting for "the one." How are you waiting for your Boaz, and what does it mean for us today?

I believe that waiting for your Boaz is first learning to love yourself right where you are and not trying to be someone else in attempting to win them or persuade them to recognize you with the intention to claim them for your own. Ruth was a servant thinking of others more than herself and willing to sacrifice to do just that to please them. She was busy being Ruth and letting God form her into a person (for us today) a person who knows who she is in Christ, her Kinsman-redeemer. It means preparation; it's a time to prepare for wifehood (ladies) or being a husband (gentlemen) and pray for them and yourself. It is never anxious; it is resting in the promise that He (God) has made. In Naomi's words: "Sit still, my daughter" (Ruth 3:18).

Boaz rises early before she does and warns his servants not to mention this to protect her reputation. Further instruction he gave to Ruth: "Bring the shawl that is on you, and hold it. And when she held it, he measured six ephahs of barley, and laid it on her" (v. 15). Six measures of barley . . . strange, engagement ring? But she waits with promise and she is being blessed in the wait.

She returns to Naomi and reports everything that Boaz had done for her and shows her the barley because he did not want her to go back to her mother-in-law empty handed. Real love—*agape'* is the Greek word for this love, which is the love of God—extends beyond the recipient at hand. In contrast, *phileo* or *brotherly* love can be just to impress the person. But real love is manifested all around. It flows from breast to breast and heart to heart, regardless of emotions, with no respect of persons. When I have God in my life, I possess this love.

Naomi, listens to Ruth's report and says, "Sit still, my daughter, until thou know how the matter will fall: for the man will not be in rest, until he have finished the thing this day" (Ruth 3:18 KJV).

The greatest manifestation to a promise is when I wait on the Lord, not the circumstances to change, but on Him.

Psalm 37:7 instructs us to "rest in the Lord, and wait patiently for Him" (NKJV); whereas, in the NIV, it says "Be still before the Lord, and wait patiently for Him." Either way, we are **to be still and rest**.

I can rest because *He* is doing the work. *I* can go to sleep because *He* never sleeps nor slumbers. I don't have to see His hand at work orchestrating the events because I trust His heart and His promises—when I wait on Him. He will not rest until He finishes the thing. It may take just a little longer than I anticipated, but I certainly don't mind because it's working for my good. *Sit still, my daughter, for the man will not rest until he has finished the thing.*

BOAZ

I think it important here to know something about Boaz. We have seen him as a man of strength. In fact, the complete meaning of his name is "strength within him." His background was not as flowery as you might think because of who he is now. We all have backgrounds and some carry baggage with it . . .

Restored Love

Boaz's Story of Love and Redemption
Pastor Patrick J. Russell

Before we look at the amazing story of Boaz and how he redeemed Ruth back into a loving relationship, we must first go back and start with the influence over his life that led him to make this God-inspired, noble decision. It all starts with a little-known Canaanite woman with a very publicly known occupation, and a decision that will bring to the forefront a loving God's redemptive plan for all mankind.

Our story starts in the 2nd chapter of Joshua that bears witness of the beginning of the downfall of the mighty city Jericho in the ancient land of Canaan. Right beyond the Jordan River lay this city, and within the mighty walls of Jericho, lived the harlot, Rahab. Rahab, a city prostitute, was well known to the men of Jericho and to the travelers that entered this mighty city. Rahab was a woman of ill-repute, yet a woman who was seeking a better life. She had a successful profession but desired a more honorable life. She was a woman living a life of desperation and one of survival but sought deliverance from this life of repression. Rahab was a woman who knew only perverted love, and most certainly experienced love lost but longed for true love that could only come from a husband and a compassionate God. Rahab was a lost woman but was also mentioned in Hebrews (11:31) as a heroine of the faith because her actions were proof of her faith.

By faith, Rahab risked her life to save the lives of the Israelite spies (See Joshua 2:1-21), and by this, saved her entire household. She chose at that time in her life to believe in Jehovah God (as did Ruth) because she had heard of the miracles done for His children.

Hearsay guided her quick thinking to take action. "Faith comes by hearing, and hearing by the word of God" (Rom. 10:17). Faith rewarded her great sacrifice. But . . . we are getting a little ahead of our story. . . . Let's take a step back into history and take up where we left off.

The scripture in Joshua tells us, again, men from the tribes of Israel were sent to spy out this great city in order to learn of its weaknesses and were intercepted by Rahab. Rahab knew who these men were, but more importantly, she knew of the One True God they served.

You see, Rahab longed for this compassionate God that redeemed Israel from the bondage of Egypt, as each person does. I call it a God-void—that place in you that only God can fill. Rahab had to long for this loving God who, in spite of Israel's failures, mercifully redeemed them from their rebellion in the wilderness, and also this resolute God who delivered and would deliver them from the hands of their enemies. Why wouldn't He?

They were God's chosen people, who once were lost, but now are found, whom He loved with an everlasting love. So, with the little faith that she had, she sought redemption (for herself and her family). By the end of the 6th chapter, we see God answering her prayer, delivering her from the destruction of Jericho, and welcoming her into the family of His people.

What some may not realize is that God's blessings and purpose did not stop with Rahab's immediate deliverance. You see, God is in the business of complete redemption and complete restoration. Yes, we all have backgrounds, and some carry not too proud baggage with it. But your past does not define your future. God takes it all and works it together for your good when you make the decision to serve Him.

41

As we now see, Rahab, a former prostitute and Gentile woman, who was instrumental in God's plans for his people and saving her family, would be lovingly welcomed into the family of God's people and would fall in love and marry a man named Salmon. He was of the tribe of Judah, the tribe that Jesus Christ, the Messiah, would come through. From this union, Rahab would give birth to none other than Boaz. (See Mat. 1:5.) So, as Boaz grew under the watchful, loving care of his mother and father, and through the testimony of his mother, he would personally learn of the redemptive nature of Jehovah God. He would learn how a loving God could fully restore one such as his mother and do so through the directed actions of man.

Again, what many may not realize is, Boaz was born and raised during Israel's initial claiming of their inheritance in the land of Canaan. Growing up, Boaz would have met Joshua, Caleb, and the other judges of that time.

More importantly, he would learn of Caleb's own story of redemption where Caleb and his Kenite family of the Edomites (lineage of Esau) would be openly welcomed in the family of God and even given an inheritance.

Boaz would also witness God's loving grace, unmerited favor, and bountiful mercies on the children of Israel and all who obeyed the commandments of Yahweh. More specifically, Boaz would learn how his mother and her family, in spite of their cultural differences, would be welcomed into the honorable family of Salmon. Boaz would learn from his father and see how he loved his mother. Finally, he would become a redeemer, who was a type of our Kinsman redeemer, Jesus Christ.

Now you can understand a little more about Boaz, who has grown to become a wealthy and influential man. And here we begin to realize his purpose.

We remember how these two women were returning from heartache, devastation, and lost love and returning without any resources, without any inheritance, and with little hope for their future. Ruth, a Gentile woman and an outsider, married against the culture and traditions of the Israelites. Ruth, if we look at it in that perspective, was also a lost woman—just like Rahab. But this did not deter honorable Boaz who, as stated before, intimately understood the value of love and redemption, the culture, and tradition.

Boaz, was a relative of Elimelech, Naomi's deceased husband. He knew of Elimelech, of his departure from Israel to Moab, and of the return of his widowed wife, Naomi. So, it did not come as a surprise to Boaz to see Naomi's ward gleaning in his fields. The foreman also gives this testimony of Ruth: "She asked me this morning if she could gather grain behind the harvesters. She has been hard at work ever since, except for a few minutes' rest in the shelter" (Ruth 2:7 NLT). That indeed caught Boaz's attention. Maybe he saw a reflection of his mother in this woman. Ruth could have reminded him of his mother's one-time insignificance and who carried the weight of a very unpopular status. He would have also reflected on how his mother was also diligent to provide for her family in spite of her status among men. In that moment of reflection, something stirs within Boaz to give Ruth more favor than even the most significant of widows who went out to glean from his fields.

Can you imagine this wealthy, influential man looking beyond Ruth's status as an insignificant foreigner and approaching her with the love and compassion that was instilled in him from God through parental instruction and personal experiences? He didn't look down on her, nor did he belittle her. Instead, he greeted her with these words: "Listen, my daughter. Stay right here with us when you gather grain; don't go to any other fields. Stay right behind the young women working in my field. See which part of the field they are harvesting, and then follow them. I have warned the young men not to treat you roughly. And when you are thirsty, help yourself to the water they have drawn from the well." (vv. 8-9). Wow! What a first liner!

As we continue to read the dialogue between Boaz and Ruth, we learn that Boaz knows who she is, but he also knows what she has done. He knows of her labels and her background, but he also knows of her diligence and compassion to others in need. He then invites her to sit down with him and his workers to eat a meal with them and then instructs his workers to make sure she gets more than just the leftovers of the harvest. The workers are to even intentionally drop some of the best of the sheaves for her to pick up and take back home. We now start to see the beginnings of a budding love that will culminate in a marriage for the ages.

Well, When Ruth delivers the news of the day to Naomi, Naomi's response opens the way for us to see Boaz's true purpose. And Naomi says, "May the LORD bless him! . . . He is showing his kindness to us as well as to your dead husband. [Naomi now tells Ruth of the relationship.] That man is one of our closest relatives, one of our *family redeemers*" (v. 20 emphasis added). But the redemption does not stop with the sustaining of two widows.

Remember, God is in the business of complete redemption and complete restoration. God moves Boaz to look at this charitable act as only the beginning of a complete blessing that will be delivered to Ruth, and for Naomi as well. As we see, although it may have been love at first sight, it took a little time for this love to fully blossom into the testimony that we still preach and teach about today. It took *Ruth's diligence and Boaz's persistence* and ultimately their obedience to restore such a love that many only dreamt about. And in the end, as we see in the 4th chapter of Ruth, Boaz makes his intentions known to marry Ruth. And this wonderful blessing is now bestowed upon Ruth: "May the LORD make this woman [Ruth] who is coming into your home like Rachel and Leah, from whom all the nation of Israel descended! May you prosper in Ephrathah and be famous in Bethlehem. And may the LORD give you descendants by this young woman who will be like those of our ancestor Perez, the son of Tamar and Judah" (Ruth 4:11-12).

What wonderful stories of love and redemption, in that we learn of a woman once lost in an oppressive lifestyle, who is introduced to a loving God and is redeemed into the hands of a loving, godly man. And another, who was once a woman disadvantaged and disenfranchised by the adverse situations in life, is redeemed into the hands of another loving, godly man, and how this is all connected. But what we truly learn is that no matter where we come from, and no matter what the mistakes of our past are, there is a loving, compassionate God who is seeking us out to redeem us and "give [us] a future and a hope" (Jeremiah 29:11). We just need to be diligent to put ourselves into position to accept His plan of redemption for our lives, our households, and those we provide for.

Yes, we all have backgrounds and some carry not-too-proud baggage with it. But your past does not define your future. God takes it all and works it together for your good. As we have seen with Boaz, in spite of his background was to be a kinsman-redeemer.

The question is now personal to you: Will you accept His love? Regardless of who you are, where you come from—to go forward in the purpose He has for you?

Chapter 6

Ruth Goes Through ... Process, Procedure, Purchase, and Promise

After Naomi's instruction, Ruth waits ... sits still, and most importantly, rests. She rests upon the promise that was given to her. Here is the question to you:

What are you waiting for, and what foundation has been given in a promise that you can *rest* upon? I think about the eternal Word of God and, of course not, people. The promise in His Word is that heaven and earth will pass away *before* one jot or tittle of His promises will ever fail. (See Mat. 5:18.)

Men may give you promises, but the promises that you can rest in are if they are based on the Word of God and confirmed by what the Lord has spoken to you.

The kinsman-redeemer goes into action as Ruth sits and rests. Boaz went to the city gate where business and legal matters were settled and sat down. Enters the close relative (redeemer) of Ruth. Isn't it interesting that Naomi, who was the biological relative, was not aware (that we know of), that there was a closer kinsman-redeemer than Boaz? Or was her choice Boaz as a better selection for

Ruth? This we do not know, but God knows every little detail of our lives that is enveloped within His purposes for us. It's all included in the process, and sometimes the process takes longer than what we think it should. But He does the unpacking of each step at a time, and each step can be a miracle. It is during this time that we will see Him working. He writes the story of our lives. Never take the pen from His hand and start your own chapter when things are not going according to the way you think they should.

There is no name of this close relative ever mentioned, but we can write our own interruptions in our lives here that happened as we were on our way towards what we thought was a straight line to our goals. And now there is another situation in our lives that slows down the process in getting to what we desire. Let's call it "a procedure." You know, it's like when you go to the doctor and after an examination, there is something unfamiliar or an irregularity found. The doctor tells you that you will have to have a procedure for a closer internal examination. After this procedure, there has to be a removal. It might be of a blockage that keeps your body from functioning the way it should. It was internal; we did not know it was there. God knew it was, but we had to go through the procedure for it to be exposed, and then it could be removed—taken care of.

Here is the same analogy with Ruth and Boaz. Internally, there was a barrier/blockage that prevented Boaz from being the one that could redeem Ruth, and it had to be exposed and dealt with first before they could continue. There was a procedure that he had to go through.

Are there some blockages in your life that are interrupting the process? What is the procedure you might need to remove something(s) that might be hindering you from receiving that which God is promising you?

He is the Specialist, the Great Physician who desires the best and will work for you. Sit still, daughter, and rest. Be willing first, and then allow the Divine Surgeon to work. We can be in denial—just ignoring what needs to be done and prolonging our wait. Are you aware and procrastinating? Procrastination is just slow disobedience to God. It is for your good and a part of His divine destiny for you. As with Ruth, God loves you so much that He has designed this very special person for you. Let Him complete the work in your life so you will be able to move forward.

After the other relative enters, Boaz invites him to come where he is using the word "friend" and for him to sit down. (See Ruth 4:1.) The procedure begins. Boaz, using wisdom and according to the traditions of legal procedures, takes ten men from the elders of the city, inviting them to sit with them, and they did also.

Boaz starts speaking to the close relative-redeemer. He tells him about Naomi, who has returned from the country of Moab and must sell the plot of land which belonged to their brother, Elimelech. We hear Boaz's integrity as he speaks, hiding nothing: "I thought I should bring the matter to your attention and suggest that you buy it in the presence of these seated here and in the presence of the elders of my people" (Ruth 4:4a). (And I like this particular wording in another version in how Boaz continues): "If you will redeem it, redeem it; BUT if not, then tell me, so that I may know; for there is no one besides you to redeem it, and I am [next of kin] after you" (v 4b AMP emphasis added).

What a great real estate and business deal is offered in honesty to this relative! Boaz, who clearly desired to marry Ruth himself, was presenting his offer in such a way that the offer of redemption would be more attractive. Following the other man's initial acceptance, it would be harder for him to withdraw.

The attraction to this business deal was immediate. Something that he did not have before would be added to what he has. The relative speaks immediately: "I will redeem it" (v 4c). And then we hear the wisdom of Boaz as he says, [by the way], "The day that you buy the field from Naomi, you must also acquire Ruth the Moabitess, the widow of the deceased, to restore the name of the deceased to his inheritance" (v 5).

You can almost hear the wheels of this relative thinking, turning, weighing out the benefits. When he learns he will also be required to redeem (also marry) Ruth, along with buying the land, he withdraws his acceptance. He replies, "I cannot redeem it for myself, because [by marrying a Moabitess] I would jeopardize my own inheritance" (v 6a). I imagine he thought while looking first at one hand and then the other: *It is not worth it. Land or this woman; my inheritance or this woman!*

Oh, but he did not know the worth of this woman. Could it be that he was holding Ruth's ethnic heritage over her proven commitment to the Lord and His people, which he, as one of all the people in the city, was undoubtedly familiar with? (See Ruth 3:11.) This is an example of true racism. This may have been the reason for his refusal to perform the Mosaic duty of a kinsman-redeemer and raise up the name of the deceased to his inheritance.

The relative says, "You redeem it yourself. I cannot do it" (v. 6c).

So many men and women also miss out on the worth of a good man or woman, weighting their decisions against their own plans, prejudices, and fears of how it may affect their goals and objectives in life. But for you that are waiting and resting, keep trusting the Lord; keep living for Him. It is all working together for your good. God's promises are not null and void for you. The best is yet to come.

The Process Continues…

The relative takes off his shoe and hands it to Boaz. Now, in earlier times in Israel, for the redemption and transfer of property to become final, one party took off his sandal and gave it to the other. This was the method or procedure of legalizing transactions in Israel. (See vv. 8-11.) It certainly saved a lot of legal fees, extended court dates and court costs, and sometimes trials. God's way has always been simple; we are the ones that complicate things. Scripture encourages us, as the people of God, to settle matters among ourselves and not take one another to court. (See 1 Cor. 6:1-6.)

Then Boaz announced to the elders and all the people, "Today you are witnesses that I have bought from Naomi all the property of Elimelek, Kilon and Mahlon, I have also acquired Ruth the Moabite, Mahlon's widow, as my wife, in order to maintain the name of the dead with his property, so that his name will not disappear from among his family or from his hometown. Today you are witnesses!—Ruth 4:9-10

Signed Sealed and Delivered!

Then the elders and all the people at the gate said, "We are witnesses: May the Lord make the woman who is coming into your home like Rachel and Leah, who together built up the family of Israel. May you have standing in Ephrathah and be famous In Bethlehem. Through the offspring the Lord gives you by this young woman, may your family be like that of Perez whom Tamar bore to Judah.—Ruth 4: 11-12

The elders not only witnessed this but spoke blessings upon this union which was to take place. Not just congratulations, but they also spoke into their generations. They spoke of double blessings that it took Rachel and Leah and their handmaidens to accomplish to produce 12 sons to build the family of Israel. And they spoke of the extraordinary circumstances that were used to carry out the will of God like that of Perez and also of Tamar, his mother, whose genealogy we do not know. She was not an Israelite, and like Boaz, her background and her life were not one to be proud of. She was a castaway but had twin sons, Perez and Zerah (by her father-in-law, Judah. See 38th chapter of Genesis.) But in all this, Perez became an ancestor of Jesus. (See Mat.1:3.) God can use the elite from the best of families and reach down and extract the castaways and use them for His glory.

The pride resulting from where you came from, or your social standing have nothing to do with your standing in God and how He desires to use you. The entitlement from who your family is, or your educational background, or your positions in life are not descriptive of your spiritual resume' in the sight of God, who determines how He can use you. The Apostle Paul, who had the most impressive resume' and biography of anyone, said that he considered his all as *dung* "for the excellency of the knowledge of Christ Jesus" (Phil. 3:8 KJV). Mentioning the background of those that have been cast aside produces shame and guilt. But neither can interfere with what God has purposed in your life when you know Jesus as Lord and Savior. Descriptive in the first few verses of Matthew are two types (Tamar and Jesus) that God used for destiny, great eternal destiny.

There is part of a praise that says it much better of your life: "In all His righteousness I stand complete in Him."

Purchased ...

Was Ruth purchased along with the land? There was nothing to dither about in looking at the traditions of that day. All that matters is that we were redeemed by the blood of Jesus, our Kinsman-redeemer, bought with a price—the great price of His life. What a great privilege and honor. Now we are free—Ruth, as we—purchased, and now free to receive the blessings. *So Boaz took Ruth and she became his wife* (4:13a).

We can look at the result of Ruth's spiritual commitment and perseverance in godliness, including her obedience to Naomi's counsel. Ruth received and experienced three additional blessings:

(1) She was taken as the wife of a godly man: "So Boaz took Ruth and she became his wife" (Ruth 4:13a AMP).

(2) Once married to Boaz, she was enabled by God to conceive: "And he went in to her and the Lord enabled her to conceive and she gave birth to a son" (4:13b). Note that in her 10 years of marriage to Mahlon, she never conceived. Psalm 127:3 speaks of children as a divine gift and inheritance and God's timing.

(3) Her conception, specifically of a son, was of special importance in biblical culture (for her) since it was the son(s) who would sustain the parents in their old age.

Let's not leave Naomi out of the blessings ...

It is so interesting that when you live a life of caring and sacrifice, the blessings overflow, and God never forgets any of the participants, no matter who they are.

I love the proceeding verses that respond to Naomi's untiring counsel and relationship with Ruth. (See vv. 14-17.) The good mother-in-law turns the curve away from the repetition of the normal definition of that word so often used negatively. Naomi is blessed for her embracing this outsider and taking her as her own as a result of her persevering focus on the will and work of God and her attending counsel to Ruth. Naomi enjoyed the blessings of having a daughter-in-law who loved her and was better to her than seven sons. (See v. 15.)

God redeemed Naomi's pain. We may experience seasons of heartache, but we can trust as we obey and follow God. He can redeem our pain. In His love and wisdom, He can make good come out of it.

Naomi was further blessed by the birth of a grandson who would be to her a *restorer of life*—a refreshing to her soul after all of the hurt and loss of her husband and two sons. He would be her *sustainer in old age* as pronounced by the women that came to see her after the birth of the baby. (See v. 15.)

As I thought about these women in attendance that came to see the baby, I imagined Naomi probably held him in her arms as they spoke into his life and hers. That would be the culmination of an awesome baby shower—instead of the clothes they quickly grow out of or the food that is served in celebration—all of that part of welcoming a baby. But to have praying women of God speak into that baby's life, covering him in prayer, is investing into his eternal purpose. After the visitation of the women, even more, Naomi became this son's nurse, an intricate part of his life.

This reaches across all cultures today as grandparents become more and more involved in the raising of their grandchildren. Some are playing a central role, together with the parents, in the daily upbringing of their grandchildren, and many all alone.

I pause to encourage grandparents. Your labor is not in vain in the Lord. He sees your efforts and your sacrifices, and you certainly will be blessed.

This child of Boaz and Ruth was named Obed, which means "servant." A chip off the old block, as we would say. He definitely was a product of his parents whose lives defined this word. Obed could have been a short version of Obadiah, which means in Hebrew "Servant of Yah or The Lord." How great to have your heritage become this! It is alright to want your children to become accomplished men and women of society, but much more than earthly accomplishments in their professions, we should endeavor, and above all desire, raising them to be simply "servants of the Lord."

The book of Ruth concludes with a genealogy. Obed grew up and fathered Jesse, who was the father of King David, a man after God's own heart. (See Acts 13:22). And again, God is in the business of complete redemption and complete restoration. For through this lineage comes God's ultimate plan for mankind's redemption. Through Salmon and Rahab, through Boaz and Ruth, through David and Bathsheba, from the virgin Mary comes Jesus Christ, the Savior of the world. Again, Wow!

Yes, establishing the lineage of David, the ideal King of Israel and providing the foundation of the Messianic line is a reminder that although Ruth, Naomi, and Boaz anticipated the birth of Obed with joy and expectation, God had greater plans, as He has for your life. The Bible reminds us "Eye has not seen, nor ear heard, nor have entered into the heart of man the things which God has prepared for those who love Him" (1 Cor. 2:9). Israel would have to wait for the son of David, Israel's ultimate Redeemer, foreshadowed by Boaz, to bring redemption for the nation.

Epilogue

Ruth, the Moabitess, is one of the few women mentioned in the genealogy of Jesus Christ. (See Mat. 1:5.) As Ruth, "I am fearfully and wonderfully made" (Ps. 139:14) . . . for purpose, although it did not appear that way at first. I experienced a lot of life's hurts and pains.

My Kinsman-redeemer, Jesus—while I was yet in my sins—came, paid a price for me, redeemed me. The One who knew no sin died in my place, rose victoriously from death and the grave—an over comer—so that I can be an overcomer of every circumstance and can have life more abundantly when I receive Him as my Kinsman-redeemer.

You know what is so wonderful? There are no insecurities. I don't have to carry any baggage from my background. Every sin has been cast in the sea of forgetfulness, never to be remembered again—in my new Life.

I am now a mirror that is to reflect my Kinsman-redeemer. I am impregnated with promises and birthing destiny. If I am, and if I know this, the question becomes, "How well am I reflecting myself in His imagine?"

He writes your story and, therefore, completes those things which concern you. Never take the pen out of His hand to write a chapter that's not a part of the story and go into another direction.

He knows us better than anyone else ever can, and still ... He loves us. When we daily surrender ourselves to Him and seek to know Him more fully, He can change our story for His glory. He's the Author who's continuing to write it.

He is in charge of your story and has great purpose for your life. His thoughts of you are for good and not evil to give you an expected end. (See Jer. 29:11 KJV.)

So, I surrender my life to Him, asking His help to trust Him when the story does not go in the direction I would like it to. But I promise you, it will all work together for your good—and even better. Just ask RUTH.

LETS RELATE THIS TO TODAY'S MAN AND WOMAN...

The Single Woman

Looking At The Single Woman In Relationship
By Mrs. Euland Rumsey Parker

We cannot go forward without speaking *of* and *to* the single woman, the many "Ruth's" that are out there with the struggles that they are experiencing. Why am I not married yet? Divorced but desiring companionship. Maybe walking in the death of a relationship but desiring companionship.

More attention and emphasis, especially in the church, is placed on ministries surrounding couples and families. At least, that's how I felt as a young adult.

For me, the story of Ruth's places of uncertainty became her place of destiny—when she left her place of comfort and familiarity. I, as so many ladies, was in a great relationship, but it was not the one God had destined me for. It was a predictable place of comfort.... It was *good*, but it was not *God*. Seems like an oxymoron; better yet, a contradiction to what the word of God says. Thinking of what my mother used to say: "It might be good *to* you but not good *for* you."

First let's look at singlehood to describe it: "Never married, or single again through widowhood or divorce." As for me, I am speaking from one that has had relationships but never married.

This journey of singleness has had many highs, lows, and many detours and turns. I was a child of a single parent, so I have experienced various levels of singleness most of my life.

As single women, we often get bogged down with the idea that our singleness is a curse or somehow punishment from God. Or, at least, that's what it can feel like when marriage is esteemed and often held at a higher level than that of the single person.

This is the feeling that I had during my early twenties—a feeling of emptiness and confusion. Here I am serving God and the people of God, a faithful member to my church and working in ministry, yet alone. Often invited to cookouts or functions, but I was reminded of my singleness when I returned home. I tried to find solace in the fact that I was a "good girl," no longer doing the things I used to do, but the more I achieved, the lonelier I began to feel. Degree after degree and promotion after promotion and no one to share it with. Lord, I don't want to die not knowing how it feels to be truly loved by a man other than my dad. Where is my Boaz?

I was 24 years old, a student, full-time employee, and a new homeowner. Life as I knew it was good for a single black girl from Queens, NY and about to get even better, so I thought. You see, one day at work, in walks this handsome, tall, slender-but-fit young man who proceeds to come in my office. Immediately, I was taken aback by his stature. "Whew, girrrllll! this MUST be it…" I thought to myself. "The Lord must have heard my cry and is answering me!" Oh, how quick we are to spiritualize something to make it "fit" our plans and desires. He introduced himself and after a few dates we made it official; I was his girl, and he was my boyfriend. After months of dating, he began *attending* church with me regularly. Our families overtime grew close—sharing holidays and momentous occasions with one another.

Materially, there was nothing that I wanted or didn't have. If I looked at it, he bought it. So, it seemed strange that after four years of dating, the feeling of dissatisfaction and the desire for more returned. Here I am with a good boyfriend but still desiring more. It was January 2013 when I began seeking the Lord for guidance. What was wrong with me?!? I am young, attractive, had a decent job, and a guy that I had fallen in love with, and he loved me. So, what happened... what was going on? Remember, I said he attended church; that's right—he wasn't saved. He did not nor did he truly desire to have a relationship with our Lord and Savior Jesus Christ. Where did I go wrong? Now, looking back over four years of the relationship, I not only confused but ignored the assignment, and he compromised my witness. I was to lead *him* to Christ but instead I allowed him to lead *me* astray. The closer he and I grew together, the farther apart I got from God. Still serving and operating in ministry but ineffective.

Now I was at a crossroad. How do I break up with someone who is seemingly good to me but not good for me? How do I answer friends, family, and even church family who had high hopes of us getting married? How do you break up with someone who is a good person? Easily... when it's not of God. It no longer became about me or him but me and God. My will versus God's will for my life. I remember my "exit interview" with him at a local restaurant two weeks before Valentine's Day. (Who breaks up with someone right before love day?!!) As I drove up to park, I knew I needed to break things off, but deep down inside, I was hoping he would say something that would change my mind... but he didn't. I went home with a sense of relief, knowing that I had done the right thing, but my heart was in pieces and my thoughts, scattered. Doing the right thing doesn't always feel good, but it will certainly work out for your good.

Here I am single again and pushing closer to my thirties. This is not how I imagined life would be, but this time things were different. I now realized that singleness is a state of being. It doesn't describe my ability, potential, purpose or personality, but it's simply a relationship status. I no longer looked at the wait as being punishment but rather preparation.

So, what do you do during your preparation season? Get before God and find out what He would have you to do. Repairing and reconciling my relationship with the Father was first on my list. How can I expect God to bless me if I wasn't living in accordance with His will for my life? It may even mean that you must ask the Lord to heal you in the hard-to-love places, the places you've been hurt and from the people who've caused you harm. Getting so involved in the things of God will cause comparison to cease and compromise to end.

Seeking God, with your whole heart, will often lead you to your secret place in Him—the hidden place, not the place of burial. So, live a life that is worth repeating, sing a song that is worth recording, and dance down the path that He has paved for you. After all, He is the best Partner one can have. Live on purpose! The purpose God has for you.

As I continued to walk with Him in holiness, this led me into deeper ministry; time for Him was all I had. I learned God will bring people into your path to mentor and walk with you. He brought several women into my life in different seasons. In fact, there was a *Naomi* in my life, and I became her *Ruth*. Ministry became a way of life and consumed every area of mine. She mentored me into the depths of ministry at home and on the foreign field. God speaks often as I found my purpose and continued to walk in it into my destiny. Yes, it's "forgetting those things which are behind, and reaching forth unto those things which are before,

I press toward the mark for the prize of the high calling of God in Christ Jesus" (Phil. 3:13-14 KJV).

And, Yes! my Boaz found me. His name—Dr. Rodney Lamont Parker. When he saw me and asked someone who I was, they told him who I was and how often I was at his church as adjutant to one of the leaders. His reply: "You mean she was gleaning in my field all of that time and I did not see her?" He became all that I wanted, plus ministry. God spoke when I prayed and said he was my destiny. After ten months we were married. God will complete those things concerning you. (See Phil. 1-6.)

The Reversal

As we pause just a minute ... I thought about how in life, there are reversals. Everything certainly is not a fairy tale. And I think it's important to talk about one now. Perhaps some are struggling with this. I believe it will set you free.

The question is: What happens when Ruth becomes the Naomi, and Naomi becomes the Ruth? **The daughter and mother reversal...** Not every mother is the Naomi of the Bible—nurturing, providing, and prayerful.

I always say "life happens to the best-laid plans." The ideal, of course, is for the mother to raise and support the daughter until she is able to support or take care of herself. But sometimes, life dishes out reversals. Along the way in rearing children, the child can become the parent, and the parent becomes the child. Sickness or circumstantial situations can reverse this order. It is with loving kindness that you can take care of and minister to the parent that has exhibited the same to you when this role is reversed, when they have shown it to you throughout your life time.

However, no parent is perfect; only Father God is. He has said to us to honor our mother and father (not just the good and supportive ones) with no strings attached. (See Ex. 20:12.) It becomes increasingly difficult when that parent is unappreciative and has made decisions in your life that were detrimental to you while you were growing up. I want to speak to those that are on that negative side.

To tell the truth, sometimes these responsibilities are thrust upon that child or adult early or at a time in their lives that it is most inconvenient. Add to that an ungrateful parent. As a child, how can you operate as the child-adult for the dependent parent? It is a sacrifice to humble yourself as the child-adult, yet be the decision maker and supporter. It becomes increasingly harder when that parent does not appreciate your sacrifice, yet feels there is an entitlement.

Integrity and devotion have always been indispensable virtues, regardless of the situation. You need to be more diligent to find and to keep your own personal inner strength and to allow it to manifest in outer actions. *Ask God to pour His love through you to them in obedience to His word.* We are to "Owe no man anything, BUT to love..." (Rom. 13:8 KJV emphasis mine). Never feel that you are obligated and they are using you. You do it as unto the Lord, and ask God to work on their hearts and yours. You cannot afford to get bitter during this season. Do it as unto the Lord, yet standing for what is right, walking in holiness, and not bowing to their ungodly personal whim. Remember, you will reap what you have sowed.

What About The Widower?

Bishop Carl A. Pierce, Sr.

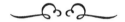

The first time I saw her, I knew she would be my wife. Don't ask me how. I just knew! Beyond her beauty, there was an essence that exuded from her that just captivated my existence.

"Man, I just saw my wife," I said to a friend who along with me had been permitted to visit the Bishop's church that Sunday night.

"Who," he said.

"That girl standing over there," I replied.

Surrounded by the saints and seemingly a host of children, she stood there clapping her hands in worship looking around at the children smiling at them as though they all biologically belonged to her. She seemed so at peace in the middle of that crowd—so where she not only *wanted* to be, but where she was *assigned* to be. I saw in her in the few minutes I beheld her a glimpse of my future as a husband and all I imagined my future wife to be. I had no idea who she was, but knew I had to find out. In fact, it seemed that possibly evening service at my church had been cancelled so that I could be at hers because destiny was even then making certain demands on my life.

Well, desiring to always make appearance at being the perfect gentleman, I dared not make a hit or move on her after service. In fact, I didn't even say anything to her personally that evening—at least, in person I didn't. But in spirit, I did indeed make connection with her and couldn't wait for the right time to say hello and formally introduce myself.

I never saw Kandace as a girlfriend, but to me she was always going to be my wife. Thus, she must be handled with care. To never be defiled. I was to not do anything that would disrespect her because she was destined to be—at least, in my thoughts—"my good thing."

Whoso findeth a wife findeth a good thing and
obtaineth favor with the Lord. (Proverbs 18:22 KJV)

After doing my research and obtaining her phone number, I can remember making the initial call, obviously not to ask her hand in marriage, but rather to get to know her and to ultimately begin to fulfill my desire for friendship. It was obvious, however, that this wasn't going to be easy because her phone demeanor in response to me testified to the fact that this wasn't the first time she had been pursued by an interested party.

"I don't think I know you," she said to me upon my initial call. And after some preliminary conversation, she had the audacity to say, "And I don't know why you're calling me, but I'm not looking for a boyfriend." To which I responded, "And I didn't call you looking for a girlfriend. I just saw you at church Sunday night, admired you, and just thought maybe we could be friends."

Friends indeed we did become. Not a lustful relationship, but a genuine friendship was developed out of which we fell in love with each other and she ultimately said yes to my proposal to be my wife.

And what a wonderful journey we enjoyed together, although not always easy, but we never allowed anything to separate us.

Her family unity was tight. Her dad and mom were seemingly inseparable, and her siblings were a close-knit clan. In fact, the night I went to ask her hand in marriage, it seemed like I had to have the entire family's yes before we could make plans for the inevitable. And notice I said *the inevitable*, because to me that's just what it was; it was inevitable that we were destined to be together.

As a child of divorced parents, I intentioned at an early age that the word "divorce" would never enter my marriage nor be a part of any disgruntled conversation.

Our marital mission statement stated that through thick and thin, we would work together to stay together, and would do everything within our power and with the help of God to honor the covenant made between us.

Having accepted my call to the ministry during the early years of our relationship, Kandace was there every step of the way from my initial sermon to my pastoral appointment and beyond. She was there and supported me wholeheartedly sparing no pain in being, first of all, my wife, but then, secondly, my companion in every ministry endeavor even as sickness invaded her body during the dawn of my episcopal elevation.

Unable to attend my consecration, she celebrated with me my promotion in the Lord's Church from her hospital bed, and awaited my return with great joy and thankfulness at what the Lord had done.

I had decided not to go to Holy Convocation because I could not imagine being consecrated to the Office of Bishop and she not be there. But with utter firmness, however, she insisted that I had to go because in her words, "This is a God thing, and your time has come for a greater level of usability in the Lord's Church."

Returning home after the consecration service the next day, I went directly to the hospital to be with her where I found her cloaked in a mixture of both joy and pain. Joyed over what the Lord had done in my life, but pained by the dis/ease in her body.

Hospitalized with a diagnosis of stage four cancer, and having undergone major surgery, she was now fighting for her life. But fighting with great faith and a courage unfathomable.

The following week, words from her doctor pierced my ears that I never imagined to hear. Words I never expected him to say to me, and words I refused to accept. Even to this day, I can recall the anger and defiance that peeked its head and raged within me.

"Mr. Pierce, I hate to have to tell you this, but as you know, your wife is very sick, and today she could expire."

"What do you mean, Doctor? For the past couple days, she's been improving, and seemingly she's headed in the right direction."

"I know, sir, but today is different. Her vitals are not looking good and something has happened and she's declining fast."

Feeling as it seemed the intensity of my pain combined with his desire, along with hospital staff, to get her through this as best they could, I saw in him that morning what I had not seen in him before, and heard what I had not expected to hear. Words I will never forget the rest of my life.

Having been hospitalized now for 30 days with a diagnosis that I was convinced that together with the help of God we could overcome because, after all, I had seen others close to us who too had the diagnosis of cancer, but God healed them and they lived. Individuals who with the various forms of treatment seemingly beat the disease and are living testaments of victory over one of the worse ills known to man.

But even as I heard those words from her doctor, I was reminded of Kandace's words just the day before as I sat on one side of the bed as the doctors stood on the other side in her room consulting with us.

"I'm a woman of faith," she said. "And I believe God. I've been taught faith and I believe. But if He doesn't do it, I'm ok, because either way, I win."

She preached to me one of my messages on faith lifting all the key points. It was so amazing to hear. The doctors shook their head in wonderment of her strong conviction and her belief in God's power to do what otherwise was beyond their ability.

That evening she slipped away. Went to be with the Lord, leaving me for One greater! That day, earth's pain became Heaven's gain. My loss became Heaven's win. And it was on that dark day, that day I took on a new title, one that I never imagined would be attached to me. I became a widower.

I always expected to go before her. Had made plans, and prided myself on preparations for her sustaining for a wonderful life after me. In fact, sitting at dinner with some of the saints one Sunday afternoon, humorously, the table talk was how and what would life be like for the survivor if God was to call either of us home before the other. Never really expecting that it would be her before me, I was not ready.

More than just a beautiful vessel of the mighty handiwork of God, Kandace was my friend, my companion, a trusted confidant, one who was cloaked with great intuition, and she possessed a wonderful spiritual gift of discernment. She was my wife, the love of my life, and she felt her calling was to be just that to me. But gone, she left me a widower thrust into the reality of a new norm. A norm of isolation and loneliness particularly as the joy of relationship was so potent.

To lose a spouse you love and cherish as a gift from God is undoubtedly amongst the most difficult challenges in life. In fact, faced with the difficult task of coping with the loss of a spouse while also dealing with the practical and emotional challenge of adjusting to life without them can indeed be a hard row to plow. Because in marriage, the two become one. Covenanted by an unbreakable union that no man shall put asunder, it is ordained of God, and intended of God to be honored until God by death does the separating.

The Scriptures declare that the Lord gives. But it also says that He takes away. And at times, in His Sovereign right and ability to exercise His will, He does just that. But amidst the healing of the grieved heart and the consolation of a heavy spirit is a confidence in God and expectation of God to always be there, and to never leave us nor forsake us, so "blessed be the name of the Lord."

Though the days of widowhood can be long and the times of loneliness severe, the feeling of grief so intense and overwhelming that it's seemingly hard to bear, yet when one is able to say that "this is the Lord's doing and it's marvelous in our eyes," it testifies to a reliance in the rule and reign of God in those things concerning us.

My spouse is gone. I am widowed, and it hurts to the core. But I thank God that I still have Jesus, who walks with me, and talks with me, and He tells me I'm His own; and the joy we share as we tarry there none other has ever known. At this juncture of life, I spend a lot of time alone, but on the other hand, I guess I'm really never alone, because I have Jesus. And I thank God for Jesus!

Coping with Widowhood . . . A Testimony

Mother Dorothy Dyett

———— ∽∾ ————

I met Elder James Dyett in March of 1964, and on June 27, 1964, we were married. The marriage lasted 54 years until he died on August 11, 2018.

He used to say, "You are going to miss me when I'm gone." I would say, "Where are you going? You are going to miss me too." As I write this, I just realized by the date on the computer that this is the third anniversary of his death, but there are days it feels like yesterday. I also realized that the statement, you are going to miss me when I am gone, was an understatement.

We went everywhere together, many times fussing, but still together (smile). Many times now, I feel like a misfit—especially around the saints who we used to fellowship with. The pain has subsided most of the time, but there is an empty space that cannot seem to be filled.

We were so different. He liked small things; I liked big things, but we learned to compromise, and as I said before—sometimes fussing.

When we first got married, I was small and he was a little heavy; and when he died, I was heavy and he was small. We never slept apart until he was in home hospice for eight months; so really, I was a widow while he lived. Oh, that was a hard time! But God gave me superhuman strength to keep my vow: "Till death do we part." When the undertaker put him in the bag, I said "Till death do we part." No one can know the pain until they have gone through it. They are nice, but they don't really know. As I write now, tears from nowhere come streaming down my face. I guess this is therapeutic (smile).

As I said earlier, I was heavy and my husband was smaller in the later years, and we always slept in the same bed. I thought everybody did until lately (smile). However, my side of the bed was lower than his, and after he passed seemed like I had to roll up a hill, which was uncomfortable. So, we got a topper—but to no avail. So the Lord spoke to me and told me to get a piece of plywood that was left over from getting a new floor put in the kitchen and put it under the topper on my side. Now, all is well; I sleep all over the bed.

Sometimes when I would be troubled and would be tossing in the bed, he would move over close and lay his hands on me, and I would go off to sleep. Sometimes it seems he still does. God is a wonder.

My husband had a big black leather chair that went up and down. I can't think of what they are called now. I had to get rid of that chair. I could not stand to look at it. People tell me I should get one; I don't ever want to see one here! If I tell the children, they would not understand. *I don't understand myself.*

I never had to keep up with my keys, or take out the garbage, or make sure the doors were locked at night. I am trying to cope with that now.

After four times, I finally got my driver's license and got my own car. Elder Dyett had sold his car and said that we didn't need two cars. So then he took me everywhere I had to go. But oh, I wish I had kept on driving, although I really didn't like it. I also don't like having to depend on people to take me everywhere. And one more thing is my husband was always on time, too. *Oh well—coping. . . .*

I miss him making up the beds for me. He used to be chief steward in the navy, and oh, could he make the bed pretty! I would lay out the bed linen and brag on him when he finished.

I hate making sure the grass gets cut, getting the gutters on the house cleaned out, checking to make sure the sump pump is working when there is a hard rain. . . . I can't seem to be able to get all of the business papers together. The children had to come over and straighten them out for me—when taking care of business and organizing was what I did before (coping).

There were hard times and good times, but because the one thing we had in common was that we loved the Lord, our marriage worked because we also loved each other. This book, as you can see, is beyond "a story." I hope it will not only cause you to think, but above all, cause you to learn lessons that will graduate you from the basics to application equaling GROWTH.

This next chapter is from one that shares with you her heart and what she has learned, not only through **widowhood**, but also in many different encounters—examples of her growth.

> *"But grow in the grace and knowledge of our Lord and Savior Jesus Christ" (2 Pet. 3:18)*

Recollections of A Long-Time Widow . . .

NO MORE TRIGGERS
Mrs. Glenda Love High

We thought it was a common case of hoarseness that would soon pass. But when it lingered a little too long, we took a trip to see the doctor. There were some tests to take, a simple procedure, x-rays to be had, specialists to see, and finally the results: advanced non-small cell lung cancer (in its 4th stage)! I wasn't familiar with the various stages and didn't know how many there were, in fact. But even hearing that dreaded "C" word, my two daughters and I did not receive it. And our immediate response was, "All is well. We got this!" Of course, the doctor was very serious when she delivered the diagnosis, but 3 out of the 4 of us didn't seem to be very concerned. We were not about to receive an evil report; as women of faith, our conviction was: "Whose report will you believe? We shall believe the report of the Lord." Reports such as "I shall not die, but live, and declare the works of the Lord (Psalm 118:17); and "With his stripes, we are healed" (Isaiah 53:5).

In reflecting on that moment, though, my husband did not show much emotion one way or the other. At first, we tried to carry on in the "business as usual" mode. However, throughout his 2-year battle and his enduring various scans, chemotherapy, radiation, multiple hospital stays, drastic weight loss, and having only a whisper of a voice, I believe he must have asked, "Why me?"

My husband was no stranger to many treatments and hospital stays for various health concerns, but generally they pertained to abdominal issues. In my mind, even the realization of his being a smoker for the many years I had known him, did not merit the sentence of lung cancer. When we first met, I smoked also. Although it was more for social reasons and to look older, I didn't really enjoy it, but it had become a habit. Then when our first daughter was almost one year old, from a Mother's Day sermon I heard, I was brought under conviction about the example I was setting for her and decided to give it up. It wasn't that hard for me to do because, as I said before, I didn't enjoy it much; however, when I was socializing, that was the most challenging time. But praise the Lord! I got the victory. Years later, when my daughter took up that awful habit, I wondered just how much she might have been influenced by my previous actions. (NOTE: Her sister, who was 3 ½ years younger, did not take up that habit.)

Within 2 years from when that evil report was made and after 40 years of marriage, I became a widow. And in the style of my husband's family, who were known for celebrating every chance they could, we celebrated his homegoing that was attended by hundreds of family, friends, and well-wishers. But one reason I could celebrate so was in knowing that my husband had accepted Jesus as his Lord and Savior just 10 days before he made his transition.

After all the festivities were over and all the crowd was gone, I was left alone in my home to unwind, relax, and reflect on the whirlwind of events that had happened in such a short period of time. Comments had been made about how strong I was and how I had held up. But when I took time to open the mail that had accumulated and I saw the check from the insurance policy, that's when the flood gates opened. The realization hit me. My husband is gone!

I tried to get on with life—adjusting to living alone for the first time; giving away some of his clothes to acquaintances; distributing some of his prized possessions to those he had instructed me to do so, and just trying to make it day-by-day. Many a night, I cried myself to sleep. I attended church faithfully, and I would cry. At any given time, I would cry, especially from various *triggers*. (I didn't know anything about triggers (other than as associated with firearms) until 11 years later, which I will expand on further into my story).

I came to learn that *emotional* triggers are events, things, experiences, or potentially people who cause the mind and body to react. (*Identifying Emotional Triggers and What They Mean*—batonrouge-behavioral.com.) Some of those triggers I remember were like when once, I was looking at TV and a character was constantly coughing while continuing to send her grandson to the store to buy her cigarettes. He was saddened when she told him she had been diagnosed with lung cancer. Another time, I burst into tears when I walked by the closet and saw a favorite suit of my husband's hanging there. There was no telling what might become a trigger.

It seems as if I cried for years, but as time went on, the tears didn't come as often. I thank God that I am a believer and can stand on His Word—that He will give me the peace that passes all understanding (Philippians 4:7) and that He will give me "beauty for ashes, the oil of joy for mourning, [and] the garment of praise for the spirit of heaviness" (Isaiah 61:3).

I often relate my marriage of 40 years to some 40-year instances in the Bible. Examples:

(1) Raining 40 days as Noah's Ark contained the only surviving members on earth. (Genesis 7:17)

(2) The Israelites wandering in the wilderness for 40 years—1 year for each day that the spies searched out the land (because of their disobedience). (Numbers 14:34)

(3) Jesus fasting for 40 days and 40 nights in the wilderness before being tempted of the devil. (Matthew 4:2)

(4) Jesus being seen on earth for 40 days after His resurrection proving by many infallible proofs that He was alive. (Acts 1:3)

Those were all examples of testing—until completion. As husband and wife, we completed our 40-year journey of matrimony together, so I guess our marriage passed the test! And although I miss my husband dearly, I feel that I have overcome this one special trigger: I am able to tell others (without crying) about the time we were sitting in our living room within the last couple of months of his life and he was able to speak in an audible voice. He said, "Thank you for loving me."

Fast forward 11 years from March 24, 2007 (when my husband died) to May 18, 2018. That was the most infamous day of my life—the day my daughter died. The year before, she had fallen upon hard times—financial woes causing the loss of her home—so she asked if she could come back home and stay with me for a while. I said yes without hesitation. It was different *returning* home after being on her own for most of her adult life. She had the upstairs, and I had the downstairs, and we shared the kitchen—if she wasn't inclined to eat out. Many years before, she had received the gift of salvation, but I sometimes questioned her choices, and, of course, that didn't sit well with her. Our lifestyles were vastly different, like being in two different worlds. We missed many opportunities to spend a lot of quality time together because often we were like two ships passing in the night with both of us doing our own thing. However, there were some good times we spent together and even shared some concerns that had previously been misunderstandings. Forgiveness was asked for and received.

Mother's Day, 2018 was approaching, and I was looking forward to my daughter attending church with me. A couple of weeks before, we had had some laughs as we were strategizing on how to prevent a mother bird from building a nest in an alcove between two columns on my front porch. In previous years, that bird—or maybe another (they all looked the same to me)—had held me hostage from coming on my own porch as she protected her young in the remarkably well-built nests she would construct. I also recalled how the bird seemed vindictive by pooping down my screen door to get back at me for trespassing on my own property! Or how she might swoop down on unsuspecting guests entering or exiting my front door. Sometimes we would have stare-downs as I would exit. So I sought to nip this nest-building practice in the bud and planned to block construction this year. It had been a battle. I would see evidence of building materials that had been dropped on the porch on the way to the construction site: some string, straw, twigs, etc. Then I'd look up and see a work-in-progress. And I would take it down and dispose of it. Next day, there would be another nest going up! Talk about persistence. . . .

Before "My #1" (endearing name my husband and I called our firstborn) went to church that Mother's Day, as we were sweeping up more building debris, we couldn't help but laugh when we caught Mother Bird mid-air in the act. She had some new material in her beak but was hesitant to deliver it when she saw us in the way. We went on to service at my church and had a blessed time. My church members knew my daughter because she had gone on various occasions to support me in my endeavors. When we returned home, wouldn't you know it! There was a hastily built, shabby-looking prefab that had been erected. It was probably the best Mother Bird could do under pressure and in such a short time. But it had to go! After that, the bird stopped building and was gone. And before the end of the week, so was my daughter.

It was Friday, May 18, 2018. I had a luncheon to attend and got up early to get ready. I didn't want to disturb my daughter's sleep because she had gotten in late the night before. I heard her when she came in but was a little peeved with her for not calling to let me know her plans, since I thought she would be home early. So instead of acknowledging her when she came in, I just remained quiet as she passed my door on her way to upstairs.

Some friends picked me up and we went on to the luncheon and had an enjoyable time. When they dropped me off back home, I didn't think much about my daughter's car still parked in front of the house. But when I went inside and didn't see her or any indication that she had stirred around in the kitchen, I proceeded upstairs and knocked a few times on her door while calling her name. After no answer, I opened the door and experienced a sense of eeriness. Something was wrong. The TV was on. Her phone was on beside her in the bed. She didn't look right. And why was she sleeping with her glasses on? I continued calling her name, shaking her, and trying desperately to awaken her, but to no avail. My heart sank as I realized her body was cold and rigid, but I refused to believe she had died in her sleep. I called 911 and the officers who responded tried to revive her. After failed attempts, the words spoken by the female officer confirmed the reality: "I'm sorry for your loss, Mam."

It's hard to make arrangements. It's now late Friday evening and we're running into the Memorial Day holiday. Her church is having special activities, and it's hard to get in touch with someone in charge because Sunday and Monday, in many cases, are non-business days for churches. And unlike before in my husband's case, I'm short one business head and set of hands because my daughter, instead of being a help, is the one homegoing arrangements must be made for. But my baby girl and a couple others come to my rescue, and we get through it with only a few hiccups along the way.

My daughter, who was so much like her father, was funeralized in the same church where he had been (with just as many or maybe even more well-wishers!) When we had gone to make arrangements at the cemetery, we had to be convinced by the cemetery representative to accept what she coined "This Miracle Grave" she was offering us. (After we had negotiated and paid for a grave a long distance from her father's grave, another grave *suddenly* became available. It just happened to be one grave up and over from her father's! And, by the way, it was less expensive than the original one we had just signed the papers and paid for. Thus "This Miracle Grave.") Look at God!

As usual, we had a blowout celebration! My daughters' friends really were a blessing and laid out the repast that we called a birthday party because my daughter passed about one month before her 50th birthday.

After all the celebrating was done and all the people gone, here come the tears. They had an even longer run than with my husband. I felt guilt, especially for not saying anything to my daughter when I heard her come in that night; nor had I checked on her the next morning before I left for my luncheon. So then come the "If only I hadda, woulda, shoulda, couldda" one-way conversations and thoughts! In addition, there seemed to take an eternity for the autopsy report to be finalized. And when I got it, it still was not acceptable to me—natural causes.

After my husband's death, the thought of going to a grief counselor never entered my mind. But when my surviving daughter saw me struggling from her sister's death, she suggested it, and I was finally convinced. (SIDE BAR: Don't be ashamed or intimidated about getting help. Don't think that as a minister of the gospel of Jesus Christ or someone with great faith that you aren't trusting God to be all you need to bring you through.) I wondered if I should go to my friend who is also a grief counselor that I had recommend to my niece three years before when her mother died. Again, with God at work, He provided me with a Christian grief counselor with great empathy, having lost her two sons to an early demise. (Yes, it was that same friend.) That's when I learned about triggers in attending the weekly sessions for a year.

One trigger that I shared at one of those sessions was this one: After the homegoing and related activities for my daughter were over, I happened to look down in the grass on my front lawn near some bushes and saw a bird sitting really still. When I approached, the bird reluctantly moved away to reveal that she had been sitting over a shallow hole in the ground made over time by driving rain flowing from my down spout. I drew closer, and what did I see inside? Two pretty blue bird eggs! Mother Bird had been denied a safe haven for her babies in a nest up high and had been driven to a dangerous low place, and I was the culprit. (Tears Fall.)

After I went inside, from my window, I saw a large predator bird swoop down. I banged on the window to shoo it away. The next day, there was only one blue egg. And the day after that, none. It hurt my heart to see Mother Bird still sitting atop that empty hole that she had been reduced to as a nest for her young. I empathized with the bird and mourned, as well. We were two mothers that had lost our offspring because we could not protect them.

Why is there so much heartbreak? Why does God allow us to go through such pain? I'm sure there are many of us who would like to advise God on a few things. But we would be wise to remember what is written in Isaiah 55:8: "For my thoughts are not your thoughts, neither are your ways my ways, saith the Lord."

I love the King James Version (KJV) of the Bible, probably because that's what I grew up on and didn't even know others existed (until adulthood). But sometimes I need to delve into the meaning and get a better understanding of Scripture, so I found myself holding on to what Paul wrote in 1 Thessalonians 5:18 (AMP): "In every situation [no matter what the circumstances] be thankful and continually give thanks to God; for this is the will of God for you in Christ Jesus." (NOTE: That's "*In*" and not "*For*" every situation!)

A portion of 2 Corinthians 1:3-5 (MSG), says this: "God of all healing counsel! He comes alongside us when we go through hard times, and before you know it, he brings us alongside someone else who is going through hard times so that we can be there for that person just as God was there for us."

God has brought me through hard times, so in sharing my experiences, I should be able to help someone else. Soon it will be 4 years since the death of my daughter and 15 for my husband. I still have pictures of both of them all around my house. They are a reminder of the good times God allowed us to have together. Instead of focusing on what I lost, I can be thankful for what I still have: a daughter in the flesh that I can love and spend time with and let her know that she is loved. And I'm going to continue to embrace words of encouragement from Philippians 4:8 that I have offered on so many occasions at many home goings:

Finally, brethren, whatsoever things are true, whatsoever things are honest, whatsoever things are just, whatsoever things are pure, whatsoever things are lovely, whatsoever things are of good report; if there be any virtue, and if there be any praise, think on these things.

I will continue to think on things of good report, that have virtue and praise. And if I can come alongside someone else who is mourning the loss of a loved one and be a blessing to them by telling them some of my story, to God be the glory. As for me, I am looking forward to the day when there will be absolutely *no more triggers!*

Thank You, Jesus. Amen.

No More Triggers Epilougue

Wouldn't you know it! After submitting my story to the author of this book three months ago and not noticing any more bird-building activity in four years, I thought my bird drama was over forever. But at the beginning of May, I saw evidence of that dreaded nest-building. My knee-jerk reaction was to halt construction—which I did. I then communicated to the author of this book my actions and intentions, but her advice was, "Embrace your Spring friends. They won't be there long." [SIDE BAR: She has been this way since we were young teenagers—always seeing the glass half-full instead of half-empty or looking for that silver lining!]

I met this with some objections and presented her with photos of proof of the ensuing extra work for me. Her reply was, "Something about that LOVE house...don't fight. Embrace this time...Stock up on Windex and enjoy the bird singing every morning for a few weeks."

Remembering how remorseful I felt before when I caused destruction to the unborn, I was conflicted and decided to grin and bear it. That was the longest month ever! Drummed up again were those memories leading up to Mother's Day, 2018—some joyful, some tearful. Birds fluttering, birds chirping, birds pooping, birds getting on my last nerve! Mix in a bout with Covid 19 causing me to miss out on holiday gatherings, prom send-offs, graduation parties, home goings, etc. and being quarantined, it's a miracle that I'm here to tell it!

Yesterday I was disheartened when I saw what I think was Mother Bird sitting comfortably on my *Back* porch. She was resistant to my shooing her away, but finally joined a group of feathered friends seeming to hunt for food. (Those baby birds had voracious appetites!)

Today when I opened my front door, there was no mean bird staring at me before taking flight and then swooping back to perch on my neighbor's ledge while observing my actions. I looked up and saw an empty nest and felt a sense of relief. Of course, I have a big clean-up job on my hands!

Welcome to the LOVE house—a different house now because of what I have learned, coupled with growth. Scripture says,

"Love is patient, love is kind. It does not envy, it does not boast, it is not proud. It does not dishonor others [even the birds!] It is not self- seeking, it is not easily angered, it keeps no record of wrongs. Love does not delight in evil but rejoices with the truth. It always protects, always trusts, always hopes, always perseveres. Love never fails" (1 Cor. 13-4-8).

And a lot of times, Love has to clean up messes. And although many times we don't understand it, we can rest on God's promise: "And we know that in all things God works for the good of those who love him, who have been called according to his purpose" (Rom 8:28).

The Holy Scriptures tell us what we could never learn any other way. They tell us what we are, who we are and how we got here, why we are here and what we are required to do while we remain here.—A.W. Tozer

The Bible Studies

References from the King James Version (KJV)

Ruth The Woman

*And Elimelech Naomi's husband died; and she was
left, and her two sons. And they took them wives of
the women of Moab; the name of the one was Orpah,
and the name of the other Ruth: and they dwelled
there about ten years. And Mahlon and Chilion died
also both of them; and the woman was left of her two
sons and her husband.*—Ruth 1:3-5

1. **How do you think the women felt at this time. Give
   some synonyms?**

God is infinite; all-knowing, omnipresent (in every place at the
same time), and present with you while you endure your mean-
time process. His foot is in the past, covering your in-between time
with redemptive love, while reaching into your future orchestrating
the manifestation of promise. Redemptive love does not remember
your past or negate your future.

2. What does that mean to you…God's foot is in your past?

3. Have you seen evidence of His reaching into your future Yes, or No…? If No…Why do you think not?

4. How do you respond when your plans don't work out or your expectations are not met?

Purpose Driven By Faith

Purpose is always woven into God's plan, and it is often through great difficulties, tests, and trials that must be experienced before you are able to enjoy the harvest. Having a sure and solid Word from God entering into any season of difficulty demands that we have faith. Even if the journey takes you into dry and desolate places void of anything tangible that resembles life, remain focused and intentional in your resolve to see the promises of God manifest in your present life. Jeremiah 29:11 reminds us,

For I know the thoughts that I think toward you, saith the Lord, thoughts of peace, and not of evil, to give you an expected end.

It is faith, the uncompromising and unmitigated boldness to trust, even when you do not have the evidence to back up what you believe, that God's plans are for your good and not evil. Faith is hope when you cannot see, and remaining committed and steadfast in your conviction in spite of what you cannot see. Deep- valley experiences will test your faith, but commitment through discipline builds Godly character and strength to endure difficulties.

5. What deep-valley experiences have you had?

6. Can you describe your feelings at that/this time?

7. What did you learn IN them?

8. Did you pass the faith test or.....?

Ruth represents a re-joining or restoration of purpose in preparation of promise and redemption through love, sacrifice, and obedience. When one season is over, a shift is required to get you from
famine to provision. The shift will not always make sense, and at
times, you are thrust into what appears to be a wilderness or spiritually dry place. Rest assured, God is with you and divine destiny
is at work!

> Whither shall I go from thy spirit? or whither shall
> I flee from thy presence? If I ascend up into heaven,
> thou art there: if I make my bed in hell, behold, thou
> art there. —Psalm 139:7-8

9. **What do you think the Psalmist meant in these verses
    as pertaining to you?**

When looking through the lens of perception, we can miss
the essence of God's favor and look past the gift or blessing. We
often abandon our processes of life when things become uncomfortable, or we lack the spiritual vision or insight to see the value in
remaining in the place of waiting. Trust is significant to faith, and
one cannot exist without operating in concert with the other. Our
disobedience does not change God's expectation or even the fulfillment of the promise, but it does change whether or not we enjoy
the fruit of the manifested promises.

*God is not a man that He should lie; neither the son
of man, that He should repent; hath He spoken, and
shall He not make it good?* —Numbers 23:19

10. Give a working definition of Trust and Faith.

11. How do you feel they work together?

**12. Can your disobedience change the fulfillment of the
promise made to you?**

**13. What words from the Scripture can you apply to your
situation now?**

Ruth, a Moabitess was a product of an idolatrous and sinful nation of ill-repute. God was with Elimelech orchestrating and weaving purpose and destiny from desolation. Moab or "of my father," where foreign gods were admonished and reverenced, was a place of spiritual desolation for Elimelech and his family.

14. Can you think of any idol god that you serve, or, better yet, lean on during your time of difficulty, ie. Money, Education? What were or are the results?

Yet there was a divine purpose for Elimelech and Naomi's family's journey. They were drawn into unfamiliar territory that would ultimately lead to the greatest act of redeeming love for mankind. Bethlehem converged dualistically with Moab at a very dark and dismal time; both were plagued with spiritual and natural desolation. The judgmental hand of God hovered over Bethlehem as a result of His children's continued disobedience and rebelliousness to the laws and His commands. The earth gave no fruit or wheat in response to sin.

Moab was sinfully debased through the practice of idol worship and human sacrifice and was inherently sinful from its beginning with incestuous roots through Lot and his daughters. (See Gen. 19:30-38.) Yet, God's unbreakable covenant with the children of Israel occurred in Moab. I want you to see the bigness of our God—with the heathen as well as His children both in sin.

Deuteronomy 29:1,12-13 states:

These are the words of the covenant, which the LORD commanded Moses to make with the children of Israel in the land of Moab… That thou shouldest enter into covenant with the LORD thy God, and into his oath, which the LORD thy God maketh with thee this day: That he may establish thee today for a people unto himself, and that he may be unto thee a God, as he hath said unto thee, and as he hath sworn unto thy fathers, to Abraham, to Isaac, and to Jacob.

15. Covenant: Naomi's sons make covenant with the Moabite women in marriage. Do you think we could do the same today? Can you see any situation that might merit it?

16. Marriage (making a covenant) with an unbeliever. Why or why not?

17. Your Bethlehem can be described as knowing to do good and not doing it. That can cause a famine in your life, physically or spiritually, etc. . . . Can you think of some? Fill in the blanks.

a) **Physically**

b) **Spiritually**

c) **Emotionally**

d) **Intellectually**

e) **Family**

For your Moab, it can mean that you never knew (as with Moab described above).

18. **For your stepping into the will of God today, take the time to list things that need to be "stepped out of" … to be delivered from.**

Trust is not rigid, but conforming and pliable, open, submitted, and willing to follow without question and with few details. With trust, comes obedience. At times, God withholds the details and only provides directives. Human behavior (flesh) demands the details before obedience, because we want to see it to believe it. This thought pattern causes stagnation and complacency.

We don't always have the answers, nor does God always reveal what is next. Complacency diminishes potential and will cause you to get stuck at the promise, never seeing the manifestation. We know this isn't the will of God. Going "through" the dry and desolate place is key to the manifestation of our purpose in the earth realm.

19. I Trust God . . . but often do not obey. Yes or No?

20. What are some areas you might be struggling in trusting God for which cause you to stumble or disobey?

21. Do you feel that it is hindering your purpose?

22. **How do you think you can go *through* them–not settle in them?**

What is trust? It is an absolute (without hesitation or question, unequivocal, and undisputable) assurance and reliance that whatever was promised will surely manifest. Trust is not based on a measure of time, and often there is a lack of substance (tangible or physical) to validate what you are trusting or believing will happen. God often gives you a Word to sustain you, comfort you, and assure you that whatever He has promised will come to pass. It is God's love for mankind and His desire that we obtain life everlasting.

Ruth willingly submitted to a life of serving Naomi, which was a sacrifice, and with compassion and love Ruth declared:

> *Intreat me not to leave thee, or to return from following after thee: for whither thou goest, I will go; and where thou lodgest, I will lodge: thy people shall be my people, and thy God my God.* —Ruth 1:16

Naomi's God changed Ruth's perspective on life. There was a divine determination to stay connected to what could be perceived as her source of life to get to the point of destiny and purpose. Barren for ten years and left without an heir to carry the family name, Ruth clung tightly to Naomi and decided to serve without promise of a future. She served while trusting blindly when nothing else remained. Ruth spoke life into her future through faith.

Without faith it is impossible to please him. —
Hebrews 11:6

23. Why is it so hard to trust God during life's "dry" season"?

24. Can you think of some areas where it appears to be dead... that you have not spoken life into?

25. How has God provided for you in the past, and how might the story of His faithfulness encourage someone you know?

The Humility of a Servant: Ruth's Submission to Naomi

26. Have you had trouble submitting yourself to a leader? Why? List some reasons?

Point to Ponder: It just might be a roadblock in your life.

Faith requires or demands commitment and diligence. God desires that we commit everything to Him without wavering so He can bless On Purpose! Everything and everyone connected to you will receive the residual blessings of favor. In the Webster dictionary, *diligence* is described as, "perseverance in carrying out an action; constant and earnest effort to accomplish what is undertaken, and persistent exertion of body or mind." Faith equates to a continual pursuit of God and seeking Him through diligence and persistence.

Now faith is the substance of things hoped for, the evidence of things not seen. —Hebrews 11:1

27. What has been your stumbling block to continue your walk with the Lord, or water down your Faith and your perseverance in carrying out a God-ordained action?

The promises of God towards you shall manifest as a witness of His grace and mercy, and also increase your faith (*Now Faith*). At the foundation of faith is *relationship*. You must first know Him, be familiar with and have intimate time with Him, and have unshakable faith and trust in Him.

SERVING IN UNFAMILIAR AND UNCOMFORTABLE PLACES (WILDERNESS)

28. What place(s) or wilderness have you found yourself in that almost seems impossible to walk with the Lord?

29. Why do you feel it so difficult to serve God there?

30. Take the time to list the ways that you <u>can have</u> this unshakeable Faith daily.

<u>Purpose</u>

How many times have you questioned your purpose in the midst of difficult and turbulent seasons in your life? The first reaction is to become *fearful* of the unknown. At times, it is painful to watch certain things play out before your eyes, and the pain can be great. I know God intimately and personally, and He has often spoken in a still and calming voice, "I am with you . . . trust Me! I will not forsake you." It is through the pain of the journey that we learn our greatest lessons.

<u>The Pain on the Journey!</u>

31. What are you journeying through now that is causing you pain?

32. **Fear can soon accompany pain before the birth of purpose. Take the time to list Scriptures here on fear and what God has to say about it.**

In the bible, "fear not" is written 144 times and is not considered a passive request but a demand. Fear is the absence of faith, and without faith we cannot please God. It is the enemy's intent to discourage, manipulate the truth of the word of God, distract, and deceive. Without a **relationship** with Jesus and being rooted and grounded in His word, we exist within our emotions (flesh) giving the enemy opportunity to take advantage of situations and circumstances intended to grow our faith in God. Enduring hardships and painful situations are opportunities for God to show Himself mighty in our lives and ignite our faith to do the impossible **if we let Him.**

On the other side of our midnight is daylight, but we must trust and have faith that God will get us to an expected (promised) end. The enemy manipulates and twists our perceptions of reality in the "wilderness" experiences by causing us to use fear as a byproduct of the process instead of using our faith. He wants our mind!

Thou wilt keep him in perfect peace, whose mind is stayed on thee: because he trusteth in thee. Trust ye in the Lord for ever: for the Lord JEHOVAH is everlasting strength. —Isaiah 26:3-4

Talk about the comfort of the Scriptures!

The Widow's Mite: A Love Story

Fear is used in an attempt to have your mind inundated or focused on memories of situations or circumstances that were painful to keep you focused on the "feelings or emotion" of the process.

> *The Lord your God he shall fight for you . . . for what God is there in heaven or in earth, that can do according to thy works, and according to thy might?*
> — Deuteronomy 3:22b, 24b

There is NOTHING too hard for God!!

These things are written for our admonition. The Word of God will overrule what fear that is in your heart and lead you into a calmness so you can be quiet to hear His voice. Learning to listen and hear His voice in the darkness trains your spiritual ear to hear in the midst of confusion meant to distract and disengage us from the will of God.

Oh, Oh here is a road bump: diversion/obstacle

What if the diversions or obstacles were a part of God's plan to get you to your expected end? God, in His infinite wisdom, love for mankind, and Creator of all things, designed our paths down to the slightest detail with intricate precision. God is the Master Architect who created the blueprint or map for your entire journey. 3 John 1:2 states:

> *Beloved, I wish above all things that thou mayest prosper and be in health, even as thy soul prosperth.*

106

Ruth was the epitome of a servant and the epitome of the widow's mite in servanthood. A servant's heart opens the pathway to divine instructions. A servant sacrifices and gives all.

You may not immediately see the blessing, but stay in purpose and do not despise your process. **Submission** is the act of yielding to a higher authority despite the circumstances and how destitute it may appear to be.

Submission is often the act of one's will against fleshy desires (fear, complacency, and lack of understanding) and coming into alignment with the will of God to experience—first spiritual, then natural—manifestations of God's promises.

33. Submission to people? Submission to a situation? Which do you find the most difficult and why?

We often release or subjugate the promise to others out of a failure to submit to the will of God. Ruth, a Moabitess and foreigner by birth, was introduced to the God of Naomi and became a Judean by marriage, accepting Hebrew customs, laws, and edicts. Without a husband or an heir, widows were deemed destitute and poverty stricken, left vulnerable to be taken advantage of, and ignored by society. Ruth was a young woman full of life and possibilities at the untimely death of her husband.

Death of a relationship

34. Has there been a death of a relationship in your life that has changed the very course of it?

35. What is/has been your response to it?

36. Taking a lesson from Ruth . . . How do you think now that it can turn around and you can move forward?

37. What are the steps to turning it around?

Abandoning Naomi and returning to Moab (place of familiarity) was customary in the absence of an heir or son. As we said earlier, Judaic laws permitted a Levirate marriage, which passed the deceased man's name and property to his son or the next available male relative. The heir had a responsibility to marry the widow and preserve the family name and heritage. And the Judaic law in Deuteronomy 25:6 states:

And it shall be, that the firstborn which she beareth shall succeed in the name of his brother which is dead, that his name be not put out of Israel.

Naomi was without a husband, sons, or an heir to fulfill the Levirate obligation and pled with Orpah and Ruth, whom she called her daughters, to turn away and leave her to a fate of sorrow at the loss of both sons, who were her hope of provision, protection, and covering. Naomi had come to terms that she would live the rest of her days alone. The following Scripture provides the backdrop of how the death of her sons, Mahlon and Chilion, was the ultimate blow that led to her despair and thrust her into a wilderness season.

And Naomi said, Turn again, my daughters: why will ye go with me? are there yet any more sons in my womb that they may be your husbands?—Ruth 1:11

38. Are you a widow, single, separated from that loved one by necessity and/or choice?

39. Has bitterness been sowed into your spirit, knotted and perennated? (*Perennate*: to live from one growing season to another, usually with a period of reduced activity between seasons.–Dictionary.com)

Your acknowledgment will be the first step before healing! Take a moment now, and tell Him all about it... confess to Him. Write your confession to make it real.

Naomi says,
Turn again, my daughters, go your way; for I am too old to have an husband. —Ruth 1:12

<u>**Lets's look at the reality of your life—what you may be going through**</u>

40. Have your feelings or the status of your life been a detriment to someone else?

41. How do you think Ruth, in the absence of a promise or covering, could trust in the God of Naomi?

SPIRITUAL AWAKENINGS AND DIVINE IMPARTATIONS BEGIN WITH YOUR

YES TO GOD

Yes to a personal relationship with Jesus Christ ... and

Building up yourselves on your most holy faith.—Jude 1:20

Faith is saying "yes" when you have no instructions or template to exist in an unknown and uncharted realm. In your weakness and frailty, God is powerful and mighty. His supernatural power keeps and sustains you in unfamiliar territory.

> *The Spirit also helpeth our infirmities: for we know not what we should pray for as we ought: but the Spirit itself maketh intercession for us with groanings which cannot be uttered.*

> *And he that searcheth the hearts knoweth what is the mind of the Spirit, because he maketh intercession for the saints according to the will of God.* — Romans 8:26-27

It is important to note that your faith must be in line with the will of God. In the absence of standing firm and believing/having faith in God's will, you waste precious time and resources in things that gratify your flesh, producing or manifesting desires without substance. It is akin to planting seeds in a ground that has been barren (unproductive and void of life), and its soil is without nutrients to sustain life. When we fail to walk upright in Holiness and forge a thorough process of sanctification, we profane the name, death, and sacrifice of the One whom we say we love— Jesus Christ! Every aspect of our being should testify to God's power of life. His redemptive love should be evident in what we do, as well as in our silent testimonies, our attitude, communication with others, and how we treat others without any expectations of reciprocated love or in-kind gestures.

> *Man is not justified by the works of the law, but by the faith of Jesus Christ.* —Galatians. 2:16a

> *He that cometh to God must believe that he is, and that he is a rewarder of them that diligently seek Him.* —Hebrews 11:6

❊ **Write a definition of Holiness and Sanctification.**

Justification is the grace and mercy shown to those who believe in God. Salvation is the faith without works.

> *For by grace are ye saved through faith; and that not of yourselves: it is the gift of God.* —Ephesians 2:8

You must first believe that Jesus Christ died on the cross, and was raised by God the Father after being "flesh" dead for three days, rising with all (irrefutable, infinite, and unmatched) power! There is no work required—only belief and acceptance.

Salvation is the beginning of relationship and learning the ways of God, recognizing His voice and His presence, and learning obedience through trust.

Trust then builds Faith!

> *[We] are kept by the power of God through faith unto salvation ready to be revealed in the last time.* —1 Peter 1:5

The redemptive work began through love, commitment, enduring the process of time, and patiently waiting for the revelation of purpose. Ruth entered Bethlehem at the exact moment predestined in the mind of God and intersected with purpose called Boaz. Ruth's union with Boaz (in Hebrew means, again, **strength** is within him) produced Obed (means "Serving and Worshipping"). Ruth became one of five significant women woven into the lineage of Jesus Christ. (See the account in Matthew 1:3, 5, 6, 16 listing Tamar, Rahab, Ruth, Bathsheba [inferred, being referred to as the wife of Urias], and Mary.)

> *. . . and Boaz begat Obed, and Obed begat Jesse, and Jesse begat David . . .* —Ruth 4:21-22

Godly character is developed and born out of difficult and arduous experiences. Keep serving until you birth your Obed!! . . .

A Widow's mite turns into . . .

Are we finished with Ruth yet? . . . Lets do a . . .

CHARACTER WORD STUDY OF RUTH:

How you can identify with her life through a relationship with Jesus Christ

Ruth is a woman of great esteem in the Scriptures, even though her background and ethnicity in the eyes of men would label her as a rejected foreigner associated with pagan worship. She was from the land of Moab; and, as a Moabitess, her culture would have made her well-versed in the worship of demonic deities like Chemosh, Baal, and many other false gods of the region. As her account unfolds in the Bible, however, we see that she is no ordinary woman. God had a plan for her and a message to communicate to us today.

Her name means "a sight" or "worth seeing," implying her beauty from a child. Subsequently, there is also another meaning to her name implying "friendship."

Proverbs 17:17 makes it clear:

A friend loveth at all times, and a brother is born for adversity.

We see this Scripture embodies exactly what Ruth is and what she does in the annals of Scripture. She emerges as a beautiful person inside and out who knows how to honor commitment as a friend. Her mettle was tested in tragedy and in her journey, but we will see her godliness shine through. Her choices, her character, and her conversion put her in position to be covered and compensated—even in a famine.

Choices, Choices, Choices

After the death of the men in the family into which Ruth married, she was left with the grieving company of her mother-in-law, Naomi, and her sister-in-law, Orpah. Being childless and without male protection was a terrible predicament for these ladies, which made being in Moab's famine seem much bleaker. Naomi makes a choice to go back to the "the house of bread" or Bethlehem in the hills of Judah, which was the country of her birth. (See Ruth 1:7.) Because our choices affect those connected to us, Naomi presents her daughters-in-law with their own choice: they could either remain in the land of their birth and remarry, or travel with her to her homeland with no guarantees of prosperity. Both women kissed Naomi—both women cried—but only one continued.

This is a great point to note: Every choice that is rational is not always right. What seems like a good option could be a missed opportunity for the blessings that can only be found in God's perfect will. Case in point, the Moabites were descendants of Lot, and we see in Genesis 13:10-13 that Lot did not have a good reputation for making good choices. Selfishness led him to choose the "better looking" parcel of land, which landed him in the gates of Sodom. Looks can truly be deceiving, and emotional decisions usually do not end well. Get beyond good looks. Pray and ask God for discernment.

Personal Points to Ponder:

+ What are the motives for the moves you are making in your relationships?

+ Are you truly willing to remain faithful in times of famine with your current connections?

+ What do you think may be some hinderances to your remaining faithful?

Conversion and Covenant

Ruth continued with her mother-in-law and makes one of the most beautiful vows ever uttered in **Ruth 1:16-17**:

And Ruth said, Intreat me not to leave thee, or to return from following after thee: for whither thou goest, I will go; and where thou lodgest, I will lodge: thy people shall be my people, and thy God my God:

Where thou diest, will I die, and there will I be buried: the Lord do so to me, and more also, if ought but death part thee and me.

Ruth makes the choice to renounce her pagan gods and put her total faith and trust in Naomi's God. She converted to Judaism at a time when a person's birthplace and religion defined them. Her choice to change religions was unheard of in her culture. You could *add* gods, but not *change* them. Similar to our culture today, the choice to be a devoted follower of Jesus Christ is becoming less favorable if you want to be in a relationship. Settling is now the norm; lowering your standards is the order of the day. You know deep down, however, it is too dangerous and too emotionally expensive to commit to superficial, uncommitted people for the sake of saying you "have someone." Choose to love God first, keep His commandments, and rest in the fact that God will always honor His Word. Ruth chose to worship and trust the true and living God. David in **Psalm 138:2** echoes:

I will worship toward thy holy temple, and praise thy name for thy ovingkindness and for thy truth: for thou hast magnified thy word above all thy name.

Being in right-standing with God through faith was the first step toward the desires of her heart. If you look closely, Ruth's pledge of allegiance to Naomi looks a lot like a vow that would be recited today in a godly wedding. . . . Read it again.

Personal Points to Ponder:

+ **Are you first completely dedicated to God through Jesus Christ?**

+ **Are you willing to throw down the idols of selfishness, status, and people-pleasing?**

+ **What are your "non-negotiables" if someone wants to be in a relationship with you? Do you need to raise your standards?**

Character Counts

Together, these grieving widows made the trek to travel over one hundred miles through the mountains. Doubtless, the climate was harsh at times. The environment was inhospitable. Predators—both animal and human—lurked, ready to consume them. It was on this path to providence that Ruth's vow was tested. Your vow will always be tested. Naomi was her guide and wisdom, leading Ruth to a place she had never been. Ruth was Naomi's strength and companion, selflessly supporting someone else's success. The lesson to learn from Ruth here is when you are in God's will, keeping your vows in the dark and unpredictable times is the real measure of true virtue. It is an indicator of ability to maintain a relationship that glorifies God. Regardless of the relationship—whether familial or romantic—your character should have an enduring quality. **1 Corinthians 13:4-8a** defines love plainly. (Emphasis mine.)

> *Charity suffereth long, and is kind; charity envieth*
> *not; charity vaunteth not itself, is not puffed up,*
> *Doth not behave itself unseemly, seeketh not her own,*
> *is not easily provoked, thinketh no evil;*
> *Rejoiceth not in iniquity, but rejoiceth in the truth;*
> *Beareth all things, believeth all things, hopeth all things,*
> ***endureth all things.***
> *Charity never faileth . . .*

Personal Points to Ponder:

+ How can you show the love of God after times of loss and difficulty?

+ Can your character (who you are when no one sees you) even handle being in a relationship right now?

+ How does the principle of sowing and reaping apply to your character?

Compensated with a King

When the pair of women arrived in Judah, no doubt they realized very quickly that life was hard for single women. Ruth decided to look for honest work (no doubt there were other kinds of "work" available for a beautiful Moabitess), and she immediately went out to take care of them both. As God's providence would have it, she selected an abundant, well-sown field to glean barley. In those days, the poor were allowed to glean on the corners of the field from what was left over.

Boaz, the owner of the field, was intentionally generous to Ruth and showed her kindness with *no strings attached*.

1. This is a good sign, is it not?

2. Everything that glitters is not gold. Ever heard that expression?

3. How would you know this was a blessing for you?

What does Professor Ruth teach us here?

She was not afraid to roll up her proverbial sleeves and work. Trade in "fairytale expectations" for taking care of natural business with good, old-fashioned, quality ministry to others with integrity. If Ruth just sat in the house with Naomi waiting to "be served," the pages to her story would be robbed of her miracle. Jesus, Himself, reminds us that He did not come "to be ministered unto, but to minister, and to give his life a ransom for many" (Mark 10:45). Boaz heard a good report, which caught his attention, about Ruth's diligence, loyalty, selflessness, and humility. He fell in love by observing her consistency in labor and hearing her testimony of devotion.

When we humble ourselves and serve the people of God, something supernatural happens for us by default. **Hebrews 6:10** encourages us:

> *For God is not unrighteous to forget your work and labour of love, which ye have shewed toward his name, in that ye have ministered to the saints, and do minister.*

There is also another important way Ruth yielded to truth. When Naomi realized Boaz was actually related to Elimelech (her deceased husband), she immediately gave wise counsel. She told Ruth:

*Wash therefore and anoint yourself, and put on your
cloak and go down to the threshing floor, but do not
make yourself known to the man until he has finished
eating and drinking.* — Ruth 3:3 ESV

Why would Naomi counsel Ruth to wash, anoint, and cover
herself? Look deeper and be instructed; it was more than just being
a pretty, shiny "trophy" for a rich man in order to get his substance.
These days, we would call that type of woman a "gold digger"—
and that honors neither the woman nor her God. Although Ruth
was poor and foreign, she was still to present herself as a stand-out
woman to be respected. Though she was not of a notable birth, she
should still have the aroma of grace, taking care to not be offensive.
She should still be free of the filth of the day; as she was clean on the
inside, she should be on the outside. She should take care of herself
and present herself with dignity, even though she was going to him
in humility. Moreover, note this: She desired his covering, but she
was not to appear desperate for it! There is nothing more off-put-
ting than that. Ruth was also to use discretion in her dealings with
Boaz. It could be argued that many potentially good relationships
end before they ever really get started because some claiming to be
"Ruths" are not **clean, anointed, dignified,** or **discrete.**

4. **Take an observation of yourself. Are you or how can
   you make sure you are clean, dignified, discrete ...
   and anointed?**

5. What are some things you may need to take off and put on?

6. Don't forget you have to <u>take off</u> . . . before you <u>put on</u>. Use the example of make-up. (See Colossians 3.)

Ruth finds Boaz sleeping after his evening meal and positions herself—not at his *side* prematurely—but at his *feet*. Pressure and desperation would have pushed this good man away. She would not let her intentions and character be misinterpreted as an "easy" and presumptuous woman. He awakens from his sleep and is startled to find Ruth making a humble request in his presence. She whispers to him, "Spread therefore thy skirt over thine handmaid; for thou art a near kinsman" (Ruth 3:9). This was an acceptable practice in that culture, and it was the petition for him to fulfil his vows to redeem, or assume responsibility for her, as her kinsman. In essence, she was saying, "We can be together if you do what it takes and pursue me the right way." That's it, Ruth; teach us! He was an older man and was honored that she would choose him in a respectable way. Needless to say, he legitimizes their love by fulfilling all the legal obligations in the presence of witnesses.

Real "Ruths" do not allow men to have them privately and then deny them publicly. Boaz made sure God was pleased with how he handled Ruth, taking responsibility for her honestly and maintaining her purity. Because of Ruth's boundaries and lifestyle, he pulled out all the stops to be her *goel*, or "kinsman redeemer." He realized she was worth it.

7. The culture at that time dictated that "he would spread his skirt over Ruth because he was a *kinsman*." How appropriate would that be today or what could we do symbolically? Or should we do anything at all?

8. What does it mean to "sit still, my daughter . . ." And rest?

9. Many of us are *sitting still* because we simply can't do anything about the situation. But write here what it means to *rest* as you sit still.

God's providence comes with our loyalty, integrity, and obedience to what is right. Naomi, Boaz, and Ruth all had reasons to celebrate because they trusted the God of the process who compensated them for their faithfulness. What became of this love story? Boaz and Ruth's union produced Obed; Obed had a son named Jesse. Why does the name Jesse sound familiar? Because he was the father of a shepherd boy turned warrior-worshiper named David—the famous giant killer, conqueror, and king. And if you look down a few more generations in the lineage of these two, you will find the King of kings—Jesus Christ, our Lord.

Ruth is an excellent example of a woman whose choices, character, and conversion glorified the God of Heaven. Those qualities made her a candidate for both His earthly and eternal blessings.

Personal Points to Ponder:

+ Am I pursuing God's anointing before I get attached to another?

+ Am I "moving too quickly" with prospective interests at the expense of my testimony?

+ Are my relationships defined, or does ambiguity leave me vulnerable to being hurt?

THE BIBLE STUDY....BOAZ...THE MAN

As we have read...Rahab, (Boaz's Mother) a former prostitute and Gentile woman would be lovingly welcomed into the family of God's people and would fall in love and marry a man named Salmon, of the tribe of Judah. From this union, Rahab would give birth to none other than Boaz (Matthew 1:5), who is the focus of this Bible Study. We agree—a wonderful outcome.

Let's review and delve again into the book in the life of Boaz . . . and see the application for our lives.

1. As we know, the name "Boaz" means: "In him is strength; My strength is in him."

Does his name exemplify his relationships & his actions with each of the following, and if so, explain how in each case:

- with the Lord
- with Ruth
- with Naomi
- with his fellow-citizens of Bethlehem

2. From our study, we know who Boaz's parents were. Is it possible that their background and experiences shaped Boaz's character and influenced his actions—especially regarding Naomi & Ruth (strong, considerate, compassionate)?

3. Does the delay in Boaz's introduction to the narrative—and to Ruth and Naomi—in any way diminish his impact and influence upon their lives? (Ruth 2:3-4)

Similarly, do the timing and circumstances of our coming to Christ limit our ability to contribute positively and eternally to the Kingdom of God? (Esther 4:14; Eccl. 3:11; II Cor. 6:2)

4. In his initial greeting to his workers, what does Boaz reveal about his relationship with God?

Concerning his attitude towards his fellow men? (Ruth 2:4)

5. There was a motive for Boaz's inquiry about Ruth's identity—what do you think it was? (Ruth 2:5-7)

6. In Boaz's first conversation with Ruth, what does he reveal about his intent toward her & Naomi? (Ruth. 2:8-9)

7. Is there insight into Boaz's attitude concerning the law of gleaning (Leviticus 23:22) from his instructions to his workers about leaving additional grain for Ruth? (Ruth 2:15-16)

8. Ruth placed herself at Boaz's feet. What does his response declare about his ethical & moral character? (Ruth 3:8-15)

9. Is there a word or phrase that best describes Boaz's actions toward his male relative, the city Elders, & Ruth? (Ruth 4:1-14)

- Decisive:

- Definitive:

- Declarative:

Let's relate Boaz to us…and we might just uncover some things…

10. Are there some <u>parent issues</u> that you have or are covering up or perhaps you might be ashamed of? … WHY?

11. As a man, what in your past life have you covered that you do not want anyone to know? … WHY?

12. What do you think would happen if you resurrected it?

13. Have you <u>forgiven </u>that parent / authority figure for what-ever happened to make you ashamed? Or for what they did to you?

14. Looking back . . . Have you shunned relationships because of your past? Or present?

15. Is there a past relationship that has hindered you from going forward?

Personal Point to Ponder

Let's think about anger/rage. Has it been a part of your life that has so consumed you that you could not make valid, conscientious decisions and move forward?

Boaz would learn from his mother about a compassionate God who is willing to change a person's situation and direct them back to the original purpose for their lives.

16. Do you know God's purpose for you?

17. Have you ventured off in another direction and set goals that have not lined up with God's Purpose for you?

18. Looking at *Boaz's persistence* to get what God had for him… Are there any areas of your life that you have gotten discouraged about, or given up on? Or where you should have been persistent?

- Take the time to list that one that comes to your mind?

- What do you think can be done about it today ....?

19. Reviewing Boaz's approach to the other nearest relative: Look at his approach. Now think of a time that you got defensive with someone. (In helping you with this, review Prov. 15:1-7, 18.)

- How did you react?

- Why do you think you reacted that way?

- How could you respond differently in God's power?

- Is it too late to seek God's will for it?

Boaz clearly "looked on the things of others (Ruth) more than himself."

20. What has God equipped you to do for those in need?

21. What does Prov. 8:34 mean to you? *Blessed is the man that heareth me, watching daily at my gates, waiting at the posts of my doors.*

Boaz would have all the tools, experiences, testimonies, witnesses, and direction needed to become that man that God had called him to be: **The Kinsman-Redeemer**.

22. Are you using that, that God has given you for His purpose for you?

Naomi, Naomi. The Widow...

1. We know how Naomi was blessed because of Ruth. If you do not have a Ruth, what are your resources?

Naomi, when she went back to Bethlehem, made this statement upon entering her home again: "Call me Mara" (which means "bitter").

2. What are your emotions now that you are a widow? List them:

   · Positive

   · Negative:

3. How can you remember the past—yet walk out of it into your new season? STEPS:

Coping:

One widow told me that she still sleeps on the side of the bed that her husband slept on with reason being so that way, her bed does not seem empty in response to her sleeping on her side only.

4. What are some things you have done to cope: negative or positive?

Naomi's grandchild—destiny wrapped up in a baby...

How do you see yours?

In the end, Naomi has a grandchild. That soothed her in the season that she had come out of (one of sadness and bitterness that she was experiencing previously). And now she was in a season of expectation. **Season of expectation . . .**

5. Have you thought about your season of expectation?

6. What expectations do you have for your life now?

7. What do you think Jeremiah 29:11 meant when he said "an expected end"... concerning YOU?

Today's grandparents are raising their grandchildren in record numbers.

8. Are you raising yours or helping to raise yours? If so ...

Do you feel there is a difference in raising your grandchildren from how you raised your children?

9. **Could this be a 2nd chance for you to be a GRAND parent?**

10. What are some struggles . . .

· **Emotionally:**

· **Financially:**

· **Physically:**

Men And Women Points To Ponder

IN THE STUDY OF THE BOOK OF RUTH

—୧୬୧୨——

Hindsight is 20/20 vision

In the words of Celia Luce:

> A small trouble is like a pebble. Hold it too close to
> your eye and it fills the whole world and puts every-
> thing out of focus. Hold it at a proper distance and
> it can be examined and properly classified. Throw
> it at your feet and it can be seen in its true setting,
> just one more bump on the pathway to life.

In other words, LIFE HAPPENS . . . and even to the best
laid plans.

My friend, Pastor Wayne Bass, says:

> Here's something terribly important to personally
> ponder. Instead of getting all bent-out-of-shape
> over anything that comes our way, we should ask
> God for perspective. Even monumental problems

eventually reach resolution or simply fade from view. When we begin to see issues and challenges as GOD sees them, we activate faith in His Word, which is tantamount to an expression of complete confidence in His plans for us.

1. Can you recall a situation that you got through...that God brought you through? Just write it down now...

2. Now (Hindsight), apply the Scriptures to it...and see it as God sees it. What could you have done differently?

3. Are you actively pursuing...Are you open to who God wants for you? Have you given Him a list of qualifications? Most importantly...Are you open to who God brings you?

Learning From Ruth, The Book

As I said before, I believe that waiting for your Boaz or finding your Ruth is first learning to love yourself right where you are—not trying to be someone else in attempting to win them or persuade them to recognize you with the intention to claim them for your own. Allow God to mold you and make you into the vessel He desires you to be.

Ruth was a servant thinking of others more than herself and willing to sacrifice to do just that to please them. She was busy being Ruth and letting God form her into a person (for us today) a person who knows who she is in Christ, her Kinsman-redeemer. Whereas, Boaz, as we know, was following his destiny for the time he would find her.

It means preparation, it›s a time to prepare for wifehood (ladies) or being a husband (gentlemen) and pray for them and yourself. It is never anxious, it is resting in the promise that He, God has made. In Naomi's words, *"Sit still my daughter"* (Ruth 3:1).

We are to *pursue* God. Many times, it will be through those that He places in our lives. Crave time in His Word (to hear from Him), and go after a relationship with Him—**our Kinsman-redeemer**—with all our heart and strength. Be a servant, even if it means *sacrificing* some of our desires in the seasons of our lives (especially in these last days) as **Ruth** did.

We are to *pursue* God in prayer. Seek Him daily. Surround ourselves with people of wisdom: "In the multitude of counsellors, there is safety" (Prov. 11:14).

Boazs are to take their places—*hearing from God, watching daily at His gates, waiting at the post of His doors*—and move into purpose, His purpose, for us . . . as men of God.

Growth is not just glad you got out of it and, perhaps, acknowledging that God delivered you, but it's also applying the Scriptures to every situation and seeing it as God sees it.

You will be able to go through every trial with confidence knowing God is in charge and it surely will work together for your good. And as Naomi told Ruth—this always rings in my spirit—*Sit still, my daughter, the man will not rest until . . . .*" Well, if He did it back then, He will surely do it again! The "on-timeiest" God is still at work—today and tomorrow and forever more. His time is always perfect!

My friends, remember that "the blessing of the Lord, it maketh rich, and He addeth no sorry with it" (Prov. 10:22).

Be continually blessed, and please (above all else) MAKE SURE YOU ARE READY TO MEET OUR SOON COMING KING, Our KINSMAN-REDEEMER!

Maranatha

Bibliography

Additional Resources

Willmington, H. L. (2011). *Willmington's guide to the Bible.* Carol Stream, IL: Tyndale House.

Holman Bible Publishers, (2009) The Apologetics Study Bible

Contributors:

Bishop Carl A. Pierce, Sr.
Pastor Patrick L. Russell
Evangelist Tekesha Russell
Evangelist Alvera Gunn
Minister Larry Bronson
Missionary Euland Rumsey Parker
Mother Dorothy Dyette
Minister Glenda Love High

Printed in the USA
CPSIA information can be obtained
at www.ICGtesting.com
LVHW041044111023
760798LV00006B/50

9 781662 884221